Recipes: The Cooking of Scandinavia

Contents

Foods of the World

TIME-LIFE BOOKS, NEW YORK

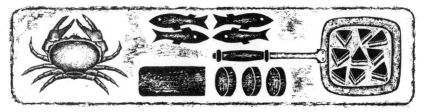

Varm Krabbsmörgås

HOT CRAB-MEAT CANAPÉS (SWEDISH)

To make 24 hors d'oeuvre

½ pound fresh, frozen or canned
  crab meat, drained, picked clean
  of shell and cartilage, and flaked
1 tablespoon dry sherry
1 teaspoon salt
⅛ teaspoon white pepper

1 tablespoon chopped fresh dill
1 tablespoon butter
1 tablespoon flour
1 egg yolk
1 cup light cream
6 slices home-style white bread

In a large mixing bowl, combine the crab meat, sherry, salt, pepper and dill
and set aside. Melt the tablespoon of butter without browning it in a small,
heavy saucepan, remove from the heat and stir in the flour. In a small bowl,
beat the egg yolk with the cream, and briskly stir this mixture into the
butter-flour *roux* with a wire whisk. Return the pan to the heat and cook
slowly, whisking constantly for a minute or two until the mixture thickens;
do not let it boil. Pour the sauce over the crab-meat mixture in the bowl
and stir together with a spoon until the ingredients are well combined.
Taste for seasoning.

Cut four rounds from each slice of bread, using a small cookie cutter or
glass. Toast the bread rounds on one side only under a moderately hot
broiler. Remove and spread the untoasted side of each round generously
with the crab-meat mixture, mounding it slightly. These may be prepared
in advance up to this point and then refrigerated. Just before serving, place
under a hot broiler for a minute or so until the canapés brown slightly.
Serve very hot.

Leverpostej
LIVER PASTE (DANISH)

To serve 12 to 16

2 tablespoons butter
2 tablespoons flour
1 cup milk
1 cup heavy cream
1 pound fresh pork liver
3/4 pound fresh pork fat
1 onion, coarsely chopped (1/2 cup)

3 flat anchovy fillets, drained
2 eggs
1 1/2 teaspoons salt
3/4 teaspoon white pepper
1/2 teaspoon ground allspice
1/4 teaspoon ground cloves
3/4 pound fresh pork fat, sliced into long, 1/8-inch-thick strips or sheets

Melt the butter in a saucepan, remove from the heat, and stir in the flour. Add the milk and cream and bring to a boil over high heat, beating constantly with a whisk until the sauce is smooth and thick. Let it simmer for a minute, then set aside to cool. Cut the liver into chunks. Roughly chop the pork fat and mix both with the chopped onion and anchovies. Divide the mixture into thirds. Purée each batch in an electric blender set at high speed, adding enough sauce to keep the blender from clogging. Transfer each completed batch to a large bowl and beat in any remaining cream sauce. (To make by hand, put the liver, pork fat, onion and anchovies twice through the finest blade of a meat grinder, then combine with the cream sauce, beating them together thoroughly.) Beat the eggs well with the salt, pepper, allspice and cloves and mix thoroughly into the liver mixture. The blender mixture will be considerably more fluid than the one made by hand.

Preheat the oven to 350°. Line a 1-quart loaf pan or mold with the strips of pork fat. Arrange the strips lengthwise or crosswise, making sure they overlap slightly and cover the bottom and sides of the pan. If long enough, let them hang over the sides; otherwise, save enough strips to cover the top. Spoon the liver mixture into the loaf pan and fold the overhanging strips (or extra strips) of pork fat over the top. Cover with a double thickness of aluminum foil, sealing the edges tightly, and place in a large baking pan. Pour into the baking pan enough boiling water to reach at least halfway up the side of the loaf pan and bake the liver paste in the center of the oven for 2 hours. Remove the paste from the oven and lift off the foil. When it cools to approximately room temperature, re-cover with foil and chill thoroughly. Liver paste may be served in 1/2-inch-thick slices as a first course, as a luncheon dish or on bread as *smørrebrød*.

Vårsmörgåsar
SPRING SANDWICHES (SWEDISH)

Makes 6 sandwiches or 24 hors d'oeuvre

½ loaf day-old homemade-type white
  bread, unsliced
10 anchovy fillets, finely chopped
4 tablespoons softened butter
2 tablespoons prepared Dijon mustard

4 hard-cooked eggs, finely chopped
¼ cup finely chopped dill, or ¼ cup
  combined dill, parsley and chives
⅛ teaspoon freshly ground black
  pepper
2 tablespoons butter
2 tablespoons vegetable oil

Trim the crusts from the loaf of bread and cut it into 12 slices ⅛ inch thick. In a small bowl, mash together the chopped anchovies, butter, mustard, eggs, herbs and pepper. The mixture should be quite smooth. Thickly spread it on 6 slices of bread. Top each slice with another piece of bread, and lightly press them together. At this point, the sandwiches may be wrapped in wax paper and refrigerated for up to 3 days or even frozen (they should be thoroughly defrosted before using).

Over moderate heat, melt the butter and oil in a 10- to 12-inch skillet. When the foam subsides, add the sandwiches, 2 or 3 at a time, and fry for 2 to 3 minutes on each side, until they are crisp and golden brown. Drain on paper towels and serve while hot, either whole as a main luncheon course or a snack, or cut in quarters to accompany cocktails.

Familjens Räddning
"SAVE THE FAMILY" HERRING PLATTER (SWEDISH)

This dish is composed of bits of food (often leftovers) often on hand in Scandinavian kitchens. It makes a pleasant cold luncheon or late-supper dish, and can also be part of the smörgåsbord.

To serve 2

2 fillets of canned *matjes* or pickled
  herring, drained
½ cup sour cream, or ¼ cup sour
  cream combined with ¼ cup
  mayonnaise
2 hard-cooked eggs, the whites and

yolks finely chopped separately
1 small cucumber, peeled, halved,
  seeded and finely chopped or ½
  cup pickled cucumbers *(page 48)*
½ cup finely chopped pickled beets,
  canned or freshly made *(page 48)*
¼ cup finely chopped parsley

Arrange the herring fillets side by side on a long chilled platter. With a sharp, heavy knife, make diagonal cuts ½ inch apart through both fillets. Spread the sour cream (or sour cream and mayonnaise) in a circle around the herring fillets. On the border of the platter, arrange alternate mounds of chopped egg white, egg yolk, cucumbers, beets and parsley.

Flaeskeaeggekage
BACON AND EGG CAKE (DANISH)

To serve 4

½ pound bacon, preferably Danish
6 eggs, lightly beaten

1 tablespoon flour
½ teaspoon salt
½ cup milk
3 tablespoons chives, finely cut

Cut the long strips of bacon in half crosswise and then fry them over moderate heat in a heavy 10- to 12-inch skillet. Do not let them get too crisp. Drain the strips on paper towels and set them on an ovenproof platter or baking dish and keep warm in a 200° oven. Remove all but a tablespoon of the clear bacon fat from the skillet.

In a mixing bowl, beat the flour and salt into the eggs only long enough to combine them, and then slowly beat in the milk. Warm the fat in the skillet over moderate heat and pour in the egg mixture. Turn the heat down to low and, without stirring, let the eggs set into a firm custard. Since this will take about 20 minutes, an asbestos pad placed under the skillet will help to prevent the bottom of the egg cake from burning. Arrange the bacon slices and chives over the top of the finished cake. Serve directly from the pan, as a first course, brunch or late-supper dish.

Fågelbo
BIRD'S NEST (SWEDISH)

To serve 4

1 two-ounce can of flat anchovy fillets, drained and finely chopped
½ cup finely chopped onions
⅓ cup capers, drained, washed, dried

and chopped
½ cup finely chopped pickled beets, canned or freshly made *(page 48)*
½ cup finely chopped parsley
4 raw egg yolks

This dish should be served on individual plates and is called a Bird's Nest *(fågelbo)* or an Eye of the Sun *(solöga)* because the ingredients are arranged around a raw egg yolk. Place 1 egg cup, cookie cutter or small juice glass in the center of each of 4 salad plates to reserve a space for the egg yolks. On each plate make a border around the glass with a thin ring of chopped anchovies, then a ring of chopped onions, one of capers, one of chopped pickled beets and one of chopped fresh parsley. The plates may be prepared ahead of time and refrigerated. Before serving, remove the glass from each plate and replace it with a raw egg yolk. Each person then mixes his own ingredients at the table. This may be served as a first course, as part of a *smörgåsbord,* or as a late-supper snack with beer.

Glasmästarsill

GLASSBLOWER'S HERRING (SWEDISH)

To serve 6 to 8

PICKLING LIQUID
¾ cup white vinegar
½ cup water
½ cup sugar

2 whole salted herring, 1 to 1½
  pounds each, cleaned and scraped,
  and soaked in cold water for 12
  hours, or substitute 4 canned
  matjes herring fillets
1½-inch piece fresh horse-radish root,
  scraped and thinly sliced, or

substitute 2 tablespoons prepared
  horse-radish, drained and squeezed
  dry in a kitchen towel
1 medium carrot, scraped and thinly
  sliced (¾ cup)
2 small onions, preferably red, peeled
  and thinly sliced (¾ cup)
¼-inch piece scraped ginger root,
  thinly sliced (optional)
2 teaspoons whole allspice
2 teaspoons whole yellow mustard
  seeds
3 small bay leaves

Bring the vinegar, water and sugar to a boil in a 1- to 1½-quart enameled
or stainless-steel saucepan, stirring constantly until the sugar completely
dissolves. Then remove the pan from the heat and let the pickling liquid
cool to room temperature.

Meanwhile, wash the herring in cold running water and cut them crosswise into 1-inch pieces. Arrange a thin layer of onions in a 1-quart glass jar
(a Mason jar, if possible) equipped with a tightly fitting cover. Top with a
few slices of herring, carrots, ginger root and horse-radish, and scatter
with some of the allspice and mustard seeds and a bay leaf. Repeat until all
of the ingredients have been used, making 3 or 4 layers.

Pour the cool pickling liquid into the jar; it should just cover the contents. Close the jar securely and refrigerate it for 2 or 3 days. Serve as an
appetizer, or as part of the *smörgåsbord*.

Soups

Spinatsuppe
SPINACH SOUP (NORWEGIAN)

To serve 4 to 6

2 pounds fresh spinach, or 2 packages
   frozen chopped spinach
2 quarts chicken stock, fresh or canned
3 tablespoons butter
2 tablespoons flour
1 teaspoon salt
¼ teaspoon white pepper
⅛ teaspoon nutmeg
2 hard-cooked eggs, sliced

Wash the fresh spinach thoroughly under cold running water to remove any sand. Drain the spinach by shaking it vigorously by hand or in a lettuce basket, then chop it coarsely. If frozen spinach is used, thoroughly defrost and drain it.

Bring the 2 quarts of chicken stock to a boil in a 3- to 4-quart saucepan and add the fresh or frozen chopped spinach. Simmer uncovered about 6 to 8 minutes, then pour the entire contents of the pan into a sieve set over a large bowl. Press down hard on the spinach with the back of a wooden spoon to extract all of its juices. Set the liquid aside in the bowl and chop the cooked spinach very fine.

Melt the 3 tablespoons of butter in the saucepan. When the foam subsides, remove the pan from the heat and stir in the flour. With a wire whisk, beat the hot stock into this white *roux* a little at a time. Return the saucepan to the heat and, stirring it constantly, bring it to a boil. Then add the spinach. Season the soup with salt, pepper and nutmeg. Half cover the pan and simmer the soup over low heat about 5 minutes longer. Stir occasionally.

Garnish each serving of soup with a few slices of hard-cooked egg. On festive occasions, such as Easter, *spinatsuppe* is often served with a stuffed egg half floating in each soup bowl. To make these, remove the yolks from 2 or 3 hard-cooked eggs (depending on how many people you plan to serve) and mash them to a paste with about 1 to 2 teaspoons of softened butter. Roll the mixture into little balls and nestle 2 or 3 into each halved egg white.

Kaernemaelkskoldskaal
COLD BUTTERMILK SOUP (DANISH)

The flavor of commercial buttermilk varies enormously from dairy to dairy. Natural fresh buttermilk, if available, would be ideal for this unusual summer luncheon or dessert soup, but cultured buttermilk of good flavor will do almost as well.

To serve 6 to 8

3 egg yolks
½ cup sugar
½ teaspoon grated lemon rind

1 teaspoon lemon juice
1 teaspoon vanilla (optional)
1 quart buttermilk
¼ cup whipped heavy cream
   (optional)

With an electric beater or a wire whisk, beat the egg yolks in a large bowl. Gradually add the sugar, beating until the eggs fall back into the bowl in a lazy ribbon when the beater is lifted. Add the grated lemon rind and juice and the optional vanilla. Slowly beat in the buttermilk, continuing to beat until the soup is smooth. Serve in chilled bowls and float a spoonful of unsweetened whipped cream on the surface of each serving if you like. Buttermilk soup is traditionally served with oat cakes *(page 67)*.

Fruktsoppa
OLD-FASHIONED FRUIT SOUP (SWEDISH)

To serve 6 to 8

¾ cup dried apricots
¾ cup dried prunes
6 cups cold water
1 cinnamon stick
2 lemon slices, ¼ inch thick

3 tablespoons quick-cooking tapioca
1 cup sugar
2 tablespoons raisins
1 tablespoon dried currants
1 tart cooking apple, peeled, cored
   and cut into ½-inch-thick slices

Soak the dried apricots and prunes in 6 cups of cold water for 30 minutes. Since the dried fruit expands considerably as it absorbs the soaking liquid, you will need a saucepan (of stainless steel or enamel) with a capacity of at least 3 quarts. Add the cinnamon stick, lemon slices, tapioca and sugar and bring to a boil. Reduce the heat, cover the pan, and simmer for 10 minutes, stirring occasionally with a wooden spoon to prevent the fruits from sticking to the bottom of the pan.

Stir in the raisins, currants and apple slices and simmer an additional 5 minutes, or until the apples are tender and offer no resistance when pierced with the tip of a sharp knife. Pour the contents of the saucepan into a large serving bowl and let them cool to room temperature. Remove the cinnamon stick, cover the bowl with plastic wrap and set the bowl in the refrigerator to chill. Serve the fruit soup in compote dishes or soup bowls as a light year-round dessert.

Ärter med Fläsk
PEA SOUP WITH PORK (SWEDISH)

To serve 4 to 6

1 pound (2 cups) dried yellow Swedish peas or substitute domestic yellow split peas
5 cups cold water
2 finely chopped medium onions

1 whole onion, peeled, studded with 2 cloves
1 pound lean salt pork, in 1 piece
1 teaspoon leaf marjoram or
   1/4 teaspoon powdered marjoram
1/2 teaspoon thyme
Salt

Wash the dried peas in cold running water and place them in a 2- to 3-quart saucepan. Cover with 5 cups of cold water and bring to a boil over high heat. Boil briskly for 2 or 3 minutes, then turn off the heat and let the peas soak in the water for an hour.

Skim off any pea husks that may have risen to the surface, add the finely chopped onion, the whole onion, salt pork, marjoram and thyme and again bring to a boil. Immediately lower the heat and simmer with the pot partially covered for about 1 1/4 hours, or until the peas are quite tender but have not all fallen apart. Remove the whole onion and the salt pork from the soup and cut the pork in slices about 1/4 inch thick.

Ärter med fläsk may be served in either of two variations. Place a few slices of pork in individual serving bowls. Season the hot soup with salt to taste, and ladle it over the pork. Or, if you prefer, serve the soup alone, accompanied by a separate plate of the sliced salt pork and spicy brown mustard.

NOTE: If domestic yellow split peas are used, they need not be soaked for an hour. Wash them carefully, cover them with 4 cups of cold water and proceed with the recipe as above. They will take somewhat less time to cook than the Swedish peas.

Kesäkeitto
SUMMER VEGETABLE SOUP (FINNISH)

The vegetables of early summer are prized in Finland, because the season is so brief. This light yet hearty soup is a favorite luncheon or late-supper main course, and the shrimp are added as a touch of luxury on special occasions.

To serve 6 to 8

4 small carrots, cut into ¼-inch
   dice (1½ cups)
¾ cup fresh green peas
1 small head cauliflower, separated
   into ½-inch buds (1 cup)
2 new potatoes, cut into ¼-inch
   dice (½ cup)
½ pound fresh string beans, cut in
   ¼-inch strips (½ cup)
4 small red radishes, halved
¼ pound fresh spinach, washed,

drained and finely chopped (2 cups)
2 teaspoons salt
2 tablespoons butter
2 tablespoons flour
1 cup milk
1 egg yolk
¼ cup heavy cream
½ pound medium-sized shrimp,
   cooked and cleaned (optional)
¼ teaspoon white pepper
2 tablespoons finely chopped fresh
   parsley or dill

Select the youngest, freshest vegetables that you can find. Wash, scrape or cut them to the sizes specified in the ingredient list. Then, except for the spinach, place all of the vegetables in a 2- to 3-quart pot, cover with cold water and add the salt. Boil uncovered for 5 minutes, or until the vegetables are just tender. Add the spinach and cook another 5 minutes. Remove the pan from the heat and strain the liquid through a fine sieve into a bowl. Set the vegetable stock and the vegetables aside in separate bowls.

Melt 2 tablespoons of butter in the pan over moderate heat. Remove from the heat and stir in the flour. Slowly pour in the hot vegetable stock, beating vigorously with a wire whisk, and then beat in the milk.

In a small bowl, combine the egg yolk and cream. Whisk in 1 cup of the hot soup, 2 tablespoons at a time. Now reverse the process and slowly whisk the warmed egg yolk and cream mixture back into the soup. Add the reserved vegetables to the soup and bring to a simmer. As soon as it comes almost to a boil, reduce the heat, add the cooked shrimp, and simmer uncovered over low heat for 3 to 5 minutes, or until the shrimp and vegetables are heated through. Taste and season the soup with the white pepper as well as additional salt if necessary. Pour into a soup tureen and sprinkle with finely chopped parsley or dill.

Bergens Fiskesuppe
BERGEN FISH SOUP (NORWEGIAN)

To serve 6

FISH STOCK

¼ cup coarsely chopped parsnips
½ cup coarsely chopped carrots
1 large yellow onion, coarsely chopped
   (¾ cup)
1 potato, peeled and chopped (1 cup)
1 teaspoon salt

6 whole black peppercorns
1 tablespoon chopped parsley stems
1 bay leaf
3 stalks of celery with leaves or celeriac
   tops
2 pounds of fish trimmings (heads,
   bones, etc.), washed
4 quarts cold water

To prepare the fish stock, which will be the base of the soup, combine the ingredients listed under that heading *(above)* in a 4- to 6-quart saucepan, casserole or soup kettle. Bring to a boil, partially cover the pan, turn the heat low and simmer for 30 to 40 minutes. Strain the stock through a fine sieve into a large bowl, pressing down hard on the vegetables and fish trimmings with the back of a spoon to extract their juices before discarding them. Wash the pan and return the strained stock to it. Reduce the stock to about 6 cups by boiling it rapidly, uncovered, for about 20 minutes. Restrain through a fine sieve or through a double thickness of cheesecloth lining a regular sieve.

SOUP

½ cup finely chopped carrots
¼ cup finely chopped parsnips
1 pound boneless halibut, cod or
   haddock, in one piece
½ cup finely sliced leeks, white parts
   only

2 egg yolks
Salt
Freshly ground black pepper
3 tablespoons finely chopped parsley
6 tablespoons sour cream (optional)

Again return the stock to the pot. Add the finely chopped carrots, parsnips and fish. As soon as the soup reaches the boil, lower the heat and simmer uncovered for about 10 minutes. Add the leeks and simmer 2 or 3 minutes longer. Remove from the heat, lift out the fish with a slotted spoon and set aside on a platter. In a small bowl, beat the egg yolks with a wire whisk; then beat in about ½ cup of the hot soup, 1 tablespoon at a time. Pour this back into the soup in a thin stream, beating continuously with a wire whisk. With a fork separate the fish into flakes and add it to the soup. Season with salt and pepper and reheat, but do not let the soup boil.

   To serve, ladle the soup into individual bowls and sprinkle with chopped parsley. If you like, garnish each serving with 1 tablespoon of sour cream.

Salads

Karrysalat
CURRIED MACARONI AND HERRING SALAD (DANISH)

To serve 6 to 8

1 small (4-inch) cucumber, peeled and
   halved lengthwise
⅛ teaspoon salt
½ cup uncooked elbow macaroni

1 pickled or *matjes* herring (2 fillets)
2 raw mushrooms, thinly sliced
2 tablespoons white vinegar
1 tablespoon olive oil
1 teaspoon salt
⅛ teaspoon white pepper

Scrape out and discard the seeds from the halved cucumber with a tea-spoon and dice the halves into ½-inch cubes. Place these cubes in a small bowl and sprinkle with salt to draw out their excess moisture. Let the cubes stand 15 minutes, then drain and pat them dry with paper towels.

Cook the macaroni in rapidly boiling salted water for 20 minutes, follow-ing the directions on the package. Meanwhile, wash the herring fillets in cold water, pat them dry with paper towels, and cut them into 1½-inch lengths. Drain the cooked macaroni in a colander, run cold water over it to cool it, then spread out on paper towels to rid it of any excess moisture.

Place the cut-up herring in a salad bowl along with the cucumber, maca-roni and sliced raw mushrooms. In a separate bowl, beat together the vinegar, olive oil, salt and pepper with a small wire whisk and pour this mixture over the ingredients in the salad bowl. With 2 wooden spoons mix the salad together thoroughly but gently. Refrigerate the salad for 1 to 2 hours before serving.

DRESSING
½ cup mayonnaise

1 cup sour cream
2½ teaspoons curry powder

DRESSING: For a richer dressing, preferred by the Danes, whip the mayonnaise, sour cream and curry powder together in a small bowl and add to the salad just before serving.

Sienisalaatti
FRESH MUSHROOM SALAD (FINNISH)

To serve 4

½ pound fresh mushrooms, in ⅛-inch
   slices
1 cup water
1 tablespoon lemon juice
¼ cup heavy cream

1 tablespoon grated onion
Pinch of sugar
½ teaspoon salt
⅛ teaspoon white pepper
Lettuce leaves

In a 1-quart enamel, glass or stainless-steel saucepan, bring the water and lemon juice to a boil. Add the sliced mushrooms and cover the pan. Reduce the heat and simmer gently for 2 to 3 minutes. Then remove from the heat, drain the mushrooms in a sieve, and pat them dry with paper towels. In a 1-quart bowl, combine the heavy cream, grated onion, sugar, salt and pepper. Add the mushrooms and toss lightly in the dressing until they are well coated. Serve as a salad, on crisp, dry lettuce.

Fiskesalat med Pepperrotsaus
FISH SALAD WITH HORSE-RADISH SAUCE (NORWEGIAN)

This salad makes excellent use of leftover boiled fish, but if you intend to use fresh, uncooked fish, prepare it according to the directions for boiled cod (page 23).

To serve 4

⅛ teaspoon white pepper

2 pounds cold boiled halibut or cod
   fillet *(page 23)*
4 tablespoons freshly grated
   horse-radish root or 4 tablespoons
   prepared horse-radish
1 pint sour cream
1 teaspoon salt

2 tablespoons finely chopped onion
1 teaspoon white vinegar
3 tablespoons finely chopped fresh dill
1 medium head lettuce, preferably
   Boston
2 hard-cooked eggs, sliced
3 tomatoes, peeled and cut in wedges

If you are using bottled, prepared horse-radish, drain it through a fine sieve, pressing out the excess juice with a wooden spoon, or squeeze the horse-radish dry in a kitchen towel or double thickness of cheesecloth. In a large mixing bowl, combine the horse-radish, sour cream, salt, pepper, onions, vinegar and 2 tablespoons of the chopped dill. Break the fish into 2-inch chunks and carefully fold it into the sour-cream dressing with a rubber spatula. Marinate for at least 30 minutes in the refrigerator, then arrange the fish, sauce and all, on a bed of dried, chilled lettuce leaves. Garnish with the sliced eggs and tomato wedges, and, just before serving, strew the remaining tablespoon of chopped dill over the salad.

Sillsallad

HERRING SALAD WITH SOUR CREAM SAUCE (SWEDISH)

To serve 8 to 10

1 cup finely chopped herring (salt, *matjes*, pickled, Bismarck)
½ pound finely chopped cooked tongue or veal (optional)
½ cup diced cold boiled potatoes
3 cups finely chopped cold beets, freshly cooked or canned
½ cup finely chopped apple, cored and peeled
⅓ cup finely chopped onion
½ cup finely chopped dill pickle
4 tablespoons finely chopped fresh dill
2 tablespoons white wine vinegar
Salt
Freshly ground black pepper

In a large mixing bowl, combine the finely chopped herring, optional meat, potatoes, beets, apple, onion and pickle. Mix three tablespoons of the dill with the vinegar, and add salt and pepper to taste. Pour over the salad ingredients and toss gently with a wooden spoon.

DRESSING
3 chilled hard-cooked eggs
1 tablespoon prepared mustard
2 tablespoons white wine vinegar
¼ cup vegetable oil
2 to 4 tablespoons heavy cream

DRESSING: Remove the yolks from the hard-cooked eggs. Mince the whites and set them aside. Force the yolks through a sieve into a small bowl with the back of a large spoon, then mash them to a paste with the tablespoon of prepared mustard. Gradually beat in the vinegar and oil, then the cream, a tablespoon at a time, until the sauce has the consistency of heavy cream. Pour over the salad, mix lightly but thoroughly, cover, and chill for at least 2 hours.

Just before serving, transfer the salad to a large serving bowl or platter and sprinkle it with the minced egg whites and the remaining chopped dill.

SAUCE
3 tablespoons beet juice
½ teaspoon lemon juice
1 cup sour cream

SAUCE: Stir the beet and lemon juice into the sour cream until it is smooth and well blended. Pass this sauce separately.

Fish

Gravlax

SALMON MARINATED IN DILL (SWEDISH)

To serve 8 to 10

3 to 3½ pounds fresh salmon, center
   cut, cleaned and scaled
1 large bunch dill

¼ cup coarse (kosher) salt, or if
   unavailable, substitute regular salt
¼ cup sugar
2 tablespoons white peppercorns (or
   substitute black), crushed

Ask the fish dealer to cut the salmon in half lengthwise and to remove the backbone and the small bones as well.

Place half of the fish, skin side down, in a deep glass, enamel or stainless-steel baking dish or casserole. Wash and then shake dry the bunch of dill, and place it on the fish. (If the dill is of the hothouse variety and not very pungent, chop the herb coarsely to release its flavor and sprinkle it over the fish instead.) In a separate bowl, combine the salt, sugar and crushed peppercorns. Sprinkle this mixture evenly over the dill. Top with the other half of the fish, skin side up. Cover with aluminum foil and on it set a heavy platter slightly larger than the salmon. Pile the platter with 3 or 4 cans of food; these make convenient weights that are easy to distribute evenly. Refrigerate 48 hours (or up to 3 days). Turn the fish over every 12 hours, basting with the liquid marinade that accumulates, separating the halves a little to baste the salmon inside. Replace the platter and weights each time.

When the *gravlax* is finished, remove the fish from its marinade, scrape away the dill and seasonings, and pat it dry with paper towels. Place the separated halves skin side down on a carving board and slice the salmon halves thinly on the diagonal, detaching each slice from the skin.

Gravlax is served as part of a *smörgåsbord* or as an appetizer, and is accompanied by mustard sauce *(page 46)*. When *gravlax* is presented as a main course, it is garnished with lemon wedges as well as the mustard sauce and served with toast and perhaps a cucumber salad *(page 48)*.

Sillgratin
HERRING AND POTATO CASSEROLE (SWEDISH)

To serve 4

3 large boiling potatoes, peeled and
    cut into ⅛-inch-thick slices
1 large onion, thinly sliced
2½ tablespoons butter

2 *matjes* herring fillets, cut in ½-inch
    diagonal slices
Freshly ground black pepper
1 tablespoon fine bread crumbs
⅓ cup light or heavy cream
1 tablespoon butter, cut into tiny bits

Preheat the oven to 400°. Place the potato slices in a bowl of cold water to prevent them from discoloring. Heat 2 tablespoons of the butter in a small frying pan; when the foam subsides, add the sliced onions and cook them over moderate heat, stirring frequently, for 5 to 8 minutes, or until the onions are soft and transparent but not brown. Set them aside.

Choose a 1- to 1½-quart baking dish attractive enough to bring to the table and, with a pastry brush or paper towels, spread with the remaining ½ tablespoon of butter. Drain the potatoes and pat them dry with paper towels. Arrange alternate layers of potatoes, herring and onions in the baking dish, seasoning each layer lightly with pepper and ending with a layer of potatoes. Pour in the cream, sprinkle the top layer with bread crumbs and dot with the bits of butter. Bring to a boil on top of the stove, then bake for 1 hour in the center of the oven, or until the potatoes are tender when pierced with the tip of a sharp knife. Serve from the baking dish.

Jansson's Frestelse
JANSSON'S TEMPTATION (SWEDISH)

To serve 4 to 6

7 medium boiling potatoes, peeled and
    cut into strips 2 inches long and
    ¼ inch thick
2½ tablespoons butter
2 tablespoons vegetable oil
2 to 3 large yellow onions, thinly
    sliced (4 cups)

16 flat anchovy fillets, drained
White pepper
2 tablespoons fine dry bread crumbs
2 tablespoons butter, cut into ¼-inch
    bits
½ cup milk
1 cup heavy cream

Preheat the oven to 400°. Place the potato strips in cold water to keep them from discoloring. Heat 2 tablespoons of butter and 2 tablespoons of oil in a 10- to 12-inch skillet; when the foam subsides, add the onions and cook 10 minutes, stirring frequently, until they are soft but not brown.

With a pastry brush or paper towels, spread a 1½- to 2-quart soufflé dish or baking dish with the remaining half tablespoon of butter. Drain the potatoes and pat them dry with paper towels. Arrange a layer of potatoes on the bottom of the dish and then alternate layers of onions and anchovies, ending with potatoes. Sprinkle each layer with a little white pepper. Scatter bread crumbs over the top layer and dot the crumbs with the 2 tablespoons of butter bits. In a small saucepan, heat the milk and cream until the mixture barely simmers, then pour it slowly down the sides of the dish. Bake in the center of the oven for 45 minutes, or until the potatoes are tender when pierced with the tip of a sharp knife and the liquid is nearly absorbed.

Keitetyt Ravut

DILL-FLAVORED CRAYFISH (FINNISH)

Scandinavian crayfish are small—about 3 inches in length—and are similar to the fresh-water crayfish of the Midwestern, Southern and Western United States. The Finns are extremely fond of these delicate shellfish and easily eat 10 to 20 apiece—usually accompanied by chilled vodka.

To serve 3 to 4

3 quarts cold water	30 live fresh-water crayfish
¼ cup salt	GARNISH
3 tablespoons dill seed	1 bunch fresh dill
3 large bunches fresh dill	Toasted white bread

In a 6- to 8-quart kettle, combine the water, salt, dill seed and 2 of the bunches of fresh dill tied with a string. Bring to a boil over high heat and boil briskly, uncovered, for 10 minutes. Meanwhile, wash the crayfish carefully under cold running water. Drop them, a few at a time, into the rapidly boiling water. When all of the crayfish have been added, cover the kettle tightly and boil about 6 or 7 minutes.

Line a 3- to 4-quart bowl with the sprigs of the third bunch of fresh dill. Remove the crayfish from the kettle with a slotted spoon and arrange them in the bowl over the dill sprigs. Strain the stock over the crayfish through a fine sieve, and let them rest in the liquid until they have reached room temperature. Then cover the bowl loosely with plastic wrap and refrigerate for at least 12 hours; they may marinate as long as 2 days if you wish. To serve, drain the crayfish of their liquid, pile them high on a platter and garnish with fresh dill. Although they can be served cold, the crayfish are at their best if they are allowed to reach room temperature. Serve with toast.

Stekt Marinert Makrell
GRILLED MARINATED MACKEREL (NORWEGIAN)

To serve 2

2 tablespoons olive oil
1 tablespoon lemon juice
½ teaspoon salt

Freshly ground black pepper
2 teaspoons finely chopped onion
2 mackerel, 1 pound each
3 tablespoons combined melted butter
   and vegetable oil

Have the fish dealer remove the backbones of the mackerel without cutting them in half. Preheat the broiler. In a shallow baking dish large enough to hold the fish laid out flat in one layer, combine the oil, lemon juice, salt, a few grindings of black pepper and the chopped onion. Place the mackerel in this marinade, flesh side down, for 15 minutes, then turn them over for another 15 minutes. Brush the broiler grill with 1 tablespoon of the melted butter and oil and place the mackerel on it, skin side down. Grill on only one side, about 3 inches from the heat, basting them from time to time with the remaining butter and oil. In 10 to 12 minutes they should have turned a light golden color and their flesh should flake easily when prodded with a fork. Serve at once, accompanied by butter-steamed new potatoes (page 50) and tomato or horse-radish butter (page 44).

Risted Laks med Kremsaus
FRIED TROUT IN SOUR CREAM SAUCE (NORWEGIAN)

To serve 4

4 fresh or frozen trout, about ½
   pound each, cleaned but with head
   and tail left on
Salt
¼ cup flour

4 tablespoons butter
2 tablespoons vegetable oil
1 cup sour cream
½ teaspoon lemon juice
1 tablespoon finely chopped fresh
   parsley

If you are using frozen trout, defrost them completely before cooking. Wash the fish under cold running water, pat them dry inside and out with paper towels, and sprinkle a little salt into the cavities. Spread the ½ cup of flour over wax paper, roll the fish around in the flour, and then shake off any excess flour.

In a heavy 10- to 12-inch skillet, heat 2 tablespoons of the butter and 2 tablespoons of oil. When the foam subsides, lower the heat to moderate and fry the trout, 2 at a time, for about 5 minutes on each side, turning them carefully with a large spatula. When all the trout have been browned, keep them warm on a heatproof platter in a 200° oven while you quickly make the sauce.

Pour off all the fat from the skillet and replace it with 2 tablespoons of fresh butter. Stir over low heat, scraping up the brown pan drippings with a wooden spoon. Add the sour cream and continue stirring for about 3 minutes, without letting the cream boil. Stir in the lemon juice and pour the sauce over the hot fish. Garnish the platter with the chopped parsley and serve at once.

Stegt Rødspaette
SAUTÉED FLOUNDER WITH SHRIMP (DANISH)

Plaice is the fish the Danes usually prepare in this manner, but flounder is an excellent American substitute. Danish shrimp are the 1-inch variety similar to U.S. West Coast shrimp. Choose the smallest fresh shrimp available.

To serve 4	2 tablespoons water
	8 tablespoons (1 quarter-pound stick)
4 fillets of flounder, ½ pound each	butter
Salt	2 tablespoons vegetable oil
Flour	½ pound small cooked shrimp,
½ cup dried bread crumbs	peeled and deveined
2 eggs	Lemon wedges

Rinse the fish in cold water and dry with paper towels. Salt lightly, dip in flour and shake off any excess. Spread the bread crumbs on wax paper. In a mixing bowl, beat the eggs together with the 2 tablespoons of water, then dip each fillet into the egg mixture and coat each side thoroughly with the bread crumbs. Let them rest for at least 10 minutes before cooking. Heat 2 tablespoons of butter and 2 tablespoons of oil in a heavy 10- to 12-inch skillet over moderate heat. When the foam subsides, sauté the fillets for 3 to 4 minutes on each side, turning them with a spatula. When golden brown, transfer the fillets to a heated platter. In a separate pan, melt 2 tablespoons of butter over moderate heat. Add the shrimp and toss them in the butter for 2 to 3 minutes until well coated. Place a line of the shrimp down the center of each fillet. Melt the remaining butter over low heat until it turns a rich, nutty brown, pour over the fish fillets, and garnish with lemon wedges. If you prefer, serve with a parsley sauce *(page 45)* in place of the shrimp and brown butter.

Fiskepudding eller Fiskefarse
NORWEGIAN FISH PUDDING OR FISH BALLS

To make an authentic Norwegian fish pudding—white, delicate and spongy in consistency—you should begin with absolutely fresh white fish. The pudding is served weekly in Norwegian homes, usually hot, with melted butter or a shrimp sauce (page 45). Cold and sliced, it is also excellent as part of an open-face sandwich.

To make 1 pudding or 60 fish balls

1 tablespoon soft butter	½ cup light cream and
2 tablespoons dry bread crumbs	1 cup heavy cream combined
1½ pounds cod or haddock, skinned	2 teaspoons salt
and boned	1½ tablespoons cornstarch

With a pastry brush or paper towel, spread the bottom and sides of a 1½-quart loaf pan or mold with 1 tablespoon of soft butter and sprinkle the mold with the 2 tablespoons of dry bread crumbs. Tip the mold from side to side to be sure that the crumbs are evenly distributed, then turn the mold over and knock it gently against a table or other hard surface to tap out any excess crumbs.

Cut the fish into small pieces and place a few pieces at a time in the jar of an electric blender, along with a couple of tablespoons of the combined light and heavy cream to facilitate the puréeing. Blend at high speed, turning the machine off after the first few seconds to scrape down the sides of the jar with a rubber spatula. Continue to blend, one batch at a time, until all of the fish is a smooth purée. As you proceed, use as much of the cream as you need, to form a smooth purée.

Place the puréed fish in a large mixing bowl, beat in the 2 teaspoons of salt and the 1½ tablespoons of cornstarch, and slowly add any of the cream that was not used in the blender, beating vigorously until the mixture is very light and fluffy. Pour it into the prepared mold and then bang the mold sharply on the table to settle the pudding and eliminate any air pockets. Smooth the top with a rubber spatula.

Preheat the oven to 350°. Butter a sheet of aluminum foil and seal it tightly around the top of the mold. Place the mold in a baking pan and pour into the pan enough boiling water to come ¾ of the way up the sides of the mold. Set the pan in the middle of the oven for 1 to 1¼ hours, regulating the heat if necessary so that the water simmers but does not boil; if it boils, the pudding will have holes. When the top of the pudding is firm to the touch and a toothpick or skewer inserted in the middle comes out dry and clean, the pudding is done.

Remove the mold from the oven and let the fish pudding rest at room temperature for 5 minutes, so that it can be more easily removed from the mold. Pour off all of the excess liquid in the mold. Then run a sharp knife around the inside of the mold, place a heated platter on top of it and, holding the mold and plate together, quickly invert the two to remove the pudding from the mold. Clear the plate of any liquid with paper towels and serve the *fiskepudding* while still hot.

TO MAKE FISH BALLS, prepare the fish in the blender as described above. Chill the puréed fish in the mixing bowl for about 30 minutes, then roll about 1 tablespoon of the fish in your hands at a time, to make 1-inch balls. Refrigerate them, covered with wax paper, until you are ready to cook them. Poach these *fiskefarse* by dropping them into 3 or 4 inches of barely simmering salted water for 2 or 3 minutes, or until they are firm to the touch. Scoop them out with a slotted spoon, drain them thoroughly and serve as part of a fish soup *(page 11)*.

Smältsill

MELTED HERRING (SWEDISH)

To serve 2

	2 tablespoons butter
1 quart water	2 tablespoons finely chopped parsley
1 teaspoon salt	3 red radishes, finely chopped or
4 medium-sized boiling potatoes,	thinly sliced
peeled	2 hard-cooked eggs, whites and yolks
2 fillets of canned *matjes* herring	chopped separately

Bring the water and salt to a boil in a 2-quart saucepan, add the potatoes and cook uncovered. Select a heatproof plate the same diameter as the pot to serve as a lid. Lay the herring fillets on the plate side by side and make neat, diagonal slices through them every ½ inch without disturbing their original shape. When the potatoes are about half-cooked (after 10 minutes or so, but test now and then with the tip of a small, sharp knife), cover the pot with the plate of sliced herring and continue cooking the potatoes over medium heat for another 10 to 12 minutes, or until the potatoes are tender and the herring is heated through, or "melted."

Meanwhile, melt 2 tablespoons of butter in a small saucepan. Cook slowly, over moderately low heat, to brown the butter lightly. Drain the potatoes, return them to their pan and dry them over low heat for a minute or two, shaking them constantly. Place the herring on a serving plate and garnish with the chopped parsley, radishes and egg whites and yolks. Pour the hot butter on the herring only and serve the potatoes in a separate bowl.

Uunissa Paistettu Hauki

BAKED PIKE STUFFED WITH CUCUMBERS AND RICE (FINNISH)

To serve 4 to 6

3 quarts boiling salted water
2/3 cup rice
1 large cucumber, peeled, seeded
 and coarsely chopped
1¼ teaspoons salt
2 tablespoons butter
½ cup finely chopped onions
2 hard-cooked eggs, coarsely chopped
½ cup finely chopped parsley
¼ cup finely chopped chives

⅛ teaspoon white pepper
1 to 3 tablespoons heavy cream
8 tablespoons (1 quarter-pound stick)
 butter
6 tablespoons dry bread crumbs
3- to 3½-pound pike, cleaned and
 scaled, with the backbone removed
 but the head and tail left on (or
 substitute mackerel or sea bass)
½ cup boiling water

Cook the rice uncovered in 3 quarts of boiling salted water for about 12 minutes, or until it is still slightly firm. Drain in a large colander and set it aside to cool. In a small bowl, toss the chopped cucumber with ¼ teaspoon of the salt. Let it sit for at least 15 minutes, then drain and pat dry with paper towels. In a small saucepan, melt the 2 tablespoons of butter and in it cook the chopped onions and cucumbers for about 6 to 8 minutes, until they are soft and transparent but not brown. Transfer them to a large mixing bowl and add the chopped eggs, cooked rice, parsley and chives. Season with the remaining teaspoon of salt and ⅛ teaspoon white pepper, and moisten the mixture with 1 tablespoon of heavy cream, adding more if the stuffing seems too dry. Mix together lightly but thoroughly.

Wash the fish inside and out under cold running water and dry it thoroughly with paper towels. Fill the fish with the cucumber-rice stuffing, close the opening with small skewers, and crisscross kitchen string around the skewers as you would lace a turkey.

Preheat the oven to 350°. In a baking dish or roasting pan attractive enough to bring to the table and large enough to hold the fish comfortably, melt the ¼ pound of butter over moderate heat. When the foam subsides, place the fish in the baking dish, raise the heat, and cook the fish for about 5 minutes, until it is a golden brown. Carefully turn over the fish with 2 large wooden spoons or metal spatulas and brown the other side. Sprinkle the top with bread crumbs and then turn the fish over again and sprinkle the other side with the crumbs. Pour ½ cup of boiling water around the fish and bring it to a simmer on top of the stove. Bake uncovered in the middle of the oven for 30 to 35 minutes, or until the fish feels firm when pressed lightly with a finger. Serve the fish directly from the baking dish.

NOTE: In Finland, 1 cup of finely chopped cooked spinach, squeezed dry, is often substituted for the cucumber in the stuffing.

Torsk med Eggesaus

POACHED CODFISH STEAKS WITH EGG SAUCE (NORWEGIAN)

To serve 4 to 6

½ cup salt

6 fresh codfish steaks, sliced ¾ inch
thick

If you don't have a long, narrow fish poacher, an enamel roasting pan 5 inches deep will do just as well. Fill the pan with water to a depth of 4 inches and add ½ cup of salt. Bring to a boil (over 2 burners, if necessary), reduce the heat slightly and gently slide the cod slices into the water with a spatula. Lower the heat until the water is bubbling slightly and simmer the fish for about 5 minutes. Be careful not to overcook or the fish will disintegrate. Remove the slices with a slotted spatula and drain them on a linen napkin or dish towel. Arrange the cod attractively on a heated platter and serve with egg sauce *(below)*.

EGG SAUCE

¼ pound butter
¼ cup hot fish stock *(from above)*
2 hard-cooked eggs, finely chopped
1 medium tomato, peeled, seeded
  and chopped
1 tablespoon finely chopped fresh
  parsley
1 tablespoon finely chopped chives

Salt
Freshly ground black pepper

ALTERNATE GARNISH
8 tablespoons (1 quarter-pound stick)
  butter, melted
1 lemon, thinly sliced
Parsley sprigs

EGG SAUCE: Melt the butter in a 1- to 1½-quart enameled or stainless-steel saucepan. Remove from the heat, beat in ¼ cup of the stock in which you poached the fish and stir in the chopped egg, tomato, parsley and chives. Add salt and pepper to taste. Heat almost to the boiling point, pour into a sauceboat, and serve with the cod. If you prefer, you can simply pour melted butter over the cod and garnish it with lemon slices and parsley. In Norway, this dish is often accompanied by raw diced carrots, sprinkled with lemon juice, and new potatoes *(page 50)*.

Poultry

Gaasesteg med Aebler og Svedsker
ROAST GOOSE STUFFED WITH APPLES AND PRUNES (DANISH)

To serve 8 to 10

8- to 10-pound young goose
½ lemon
Salt
Freshly ground black pepper

2 cups apples, peeled, cored and
    coarsely chopped
2 cups presoaked dried prunes, pitted
    and chopped
1 large onion, peeled and quartered

Preheat the oven to 325°. To prepare this classic Danish Christmas dish, first wash the goose under cold running water. Pat it thoroughly dry with paper towels, then rub the bird inside and out with the cut side of half a lemon. Lightly salt and pepper the inside, and stuff the cavity with the coarsely chopped apples and prunes and the onion quarters. Close the opening by lacing it with skewers or by sewing it with heavy white thread. Fasten the neck skin to the back of the goose with a skewer and truss the bird securely so that it will keep its shape while cooking.

Roast the goose on a rack set in a shallow open pan for 3 to 3½ hours (about 20 to 25 minutes to the pound). As the goose fat accumulates in the pan, draw it off with a bulb baster or large kitchen spoon. Basting the goose itself is unnecessary.

To test whether the bird is done, pierce the thigh with the tip of a small, sharp knife. If the juice that runs out is still somewhat pink, roast another 5 to 10 minutes. If the juice is a pale yellow, set the finished bird in the turned-off oven with the door ajar for about 15 minutes to make it easier to carve.

Transfer the goose to a large heated platter and remove the string and skewers. Scoop out the stuffing and discard it. The fruits and onion will have imparted their flavor to the goose but will be far too fatty to serve.

Traditionally, poached apples stuffed with prunes *(page 47)* are served with the Christmas goose. Red cabbage and caramelized potatoes *(pages 51 and 49)* complete the Christmas menu in Denmark.

Stegt Kylling
BRAISED CHICKEN WITH PARSLEY (DANISH)

To serve 4

	Large bunch of parsley
3- to 3½-pound roasting chicken	2 tablespoons butter
1 tablespoon salt	¼ cup vegetable oil
8 tablespoons (1 quarter-pound stick)	½ cup water
butter, softened	1 cup heavy cream

Pat the chicken dry with paper towels, then rub it thoroughly inside and out with salt. Cream the ¼ pound of butter by using an electric mixer set at medium speed or by beating it vigorously against the side of a bowl with a wooden spoon. With a pastry brush or your fingers, spread it inside the chicken. Then stuff the chicken with the entire bunch of parsley, and truss it so that it will hold its shape while cooking.

Preheat the oven to 325°. Heat the 2 tablespoons of butter and the oil over moderate heat on top of the stove in a heavy flameproof casserole or a roasting pan just large enough to hold the chicken comfortably, and put the chicken in breast side down. After about 5 minutes, turn the bird on its side, holding it with two large wooden spoons or a kitchen towel to avoid breaking the skin. In another 5 to 10 minutes, when this side is sufficiently browned, turn the chicken on its other side, then finally on its back for 5 minutes or so. The browning of the chicken should take about 20 minutes in all.

Transfer the chicken to a platter and pour off all but about 1 tablespoon of fat from the casserole. In its place, add ½ cup of water and bring it to a boil, stirring vigorously to scrape up any browned bits clinging to the pan. Return the chicken to the casserole, breast side up, cover it tightly and place the casserole in the oven to braise for about 1 hour. To test, lift the chicken upright out of the pan with a wooden spoon inserted in the tail opening. If the juice that runs out is yellow, the chicken is done; if still somewhat pink, braise the chicken another 5 to 10 minutes.

Place the chicken on a carving board and let it rest for 5 minutes or so while you make the sauce. Skim and discard the fat from the pan juices, add the cream and bring to a boil, stirring rapidly and scraping up any browned bits in the bottom and sides of the pan. Boil the sauce briskly for several minutes, until the cream has reduced and the sauce thickens. Taste for seasoning, add more salt if needed, and pour the sauce into a heated sauceboat.

Boiled new potatoes and cucumber salad *(page 48)* are often served with *stegt kylling*.

Meats

Äppel-Fläsk

SMOKED BACON WITH ONIONS AND APPLE RINGS (SWEDISH)

To serve 4

2 to 4 tablespoons butter
1 pound Canadian bacon
2 large red, tart cooking apples,
unpeeled, cored and cut in
½-inch-thick rings
2 large onions, thinly sliced
Freshly ground black pepper

Melt 2 tablespoons of butter in a heavy 10- to 12-inch skillet, and when the foam subsides, add the bacon. Fry 5 to 10 minutes, or until the bacon is lightly browned. Remove from the skillet with a slotted spatula and set aside on paper towels to drain.

Fry the onion slices for 6 to 8 minutes in the fat remaining in the skillet, adding more butter if necessary. When the onions are soft and transparent, add the apple rings and cover the pan. Simmer over low heat for 5 to 10 minutes, shaking the pan gently at intervals to prevent the apples from sticking.

When the apple rings are sufficiently cooked (they should offer little or no resistance when pierced with the tip of a sharp knife), return the drained bacon to the skillet. Cover the pan and simmer an additional 3 to 5 minutes, or until the bacon is heated through. Grind black pepper liberally over the top and serve the *äppel-fläsk* directly from the pan as a luncheon entrée or Sunday night supper.

Dyrestek
ROAST VENISON (OR REINDEER) WITH GOAT-CHEESE SAUCE (NORWEGIAN)

To serve 6 to 8

3½ pounds boneless haunch of
    venison or reindeer
3 tablespoons butter, softened
Salt
Freshly ground black pepper

1⅓ cups beef stock
1 tablespoon butter
1 tablespoon flour
2 teaspoons red currant jelly
½ ounce brown Norwegian goat
    cheese (Gjetöst), finely diced
½ cup sour cream

Preheat the oven to 475°. Tie the roast up neatly at ½-inch intervals with kitchen cord so that it will hold its shape while cooking. With a pastry brush, spread the softened butter evenly over the meat. Place the roast on a rack in a shallow open roasting pan and sear it in the hot oven for about 20 minutes. When the surface of the meat is quite brown, reduce the heat to 375° and sprinkle the roast generously with salt and a few grindings of pepper. Pour the stock into the pan and cook the roast, uncovered, for 1¼ hours. With a large spoon or bulb baster, baste the meat with the pan juices every half hour or so. The interior meat, when finished, should be slightly rare, or about 150° on a meat thermometer. Remove the roast to a heated platter, cover it loosely with foil and let it rest in the turned-off oven while you make the sauce.

Skim and discard the fat from the pan juices. Measure the remaining liquid and either reduce to 1 cup by boiling it rapidly or add enough water to make up 1 cup. In a small, heavy saucepan, heat 1 tablespoon of butter and stir in 1 tablespoon of flour. Stirring continuously with a wooden spoon, cook this *roux* for 6 to 8 minutes over low heat until it is a nut-brown color. Be careful not to let it burn or it will give the sauce a bitter flavor. Now, with a wire whisk, beat the pan juices into the *roux*. Next whisk in the jelly and the cheese. Beat until they dissolve and the sauce is absolutely smooth, then stir in the sour cream. Do not allow the sauce to boil. Taste for seasoning, remove the strings from the roast, and carve the meat in thin slices. Pass the sauce separately.

Mørbrad med Svedsker og Aebler

PORK LOIN STUFFED WITH PRUNES AND APPLES (DANISH)

To serve 6 to 8

4½- to 5-pound boned loin of pork,
  center cut
12 medium-sized pitted prunes
1 large tart apple, peeled, cored and
  cut into 1-inch cubes
1 teaspoon lemon juice

Salt
Freshly ground black pepper
3 tablespoons butter
3 tablespoons vegetable oil
¾ cup dry white wine
¾ cup heavy cream
1 tablespoon red currant jelly

Place the prunes in a saucepan, cover with cold water, and bring to a boil. Remove from the heat and let the prunes soak in the water for 30 minutes. Then drain, pat dry with paper towels, and set aside. Sprinkle the cubed apple with lemon juice to prevent discoloring. With a strong, sharp knife, make a pocket in the pork by cutting a deep slit down the length of the loin, going to within ½ inch of the two ends and to within 1 inch of the other side. Season the pocket lightly with salt and pepper and stuff it with the prunes and apples, sewing up the opening with strong kitchen thread. Tie the loin at 1-inch intervals to keep its shape while cooking.

Preheat the oven to 350°. In a casserole equipped with a cover and just large enough to hold the loin of pork comfortably, melt the butter and oil over moderate heat. When the foam subsides, add the loin, turning it from time to time with 2 wooden spoons. It should take about 20 minutes to brown the loin evenly on all sides. With a bulb baster or large spoon, remove all the fat from the pan. Pour in the wine, stir in the heavy cream, whisking briskly, and bring to a simmer on top of the stove. Cover the pan and cook in the center of the oven for 1½ hours, or until the meat shows no resistance when pierced with the tip of a sharp knife.

Remove the loin from the pan and let it rest on a heated platter while you finish the sauce. Skim the fat from the liquid in the pan and bring the liquid to a boil. When it has reduced to about 1 cup, stir in the red currant jelly, reduce the heat and, stirring constantly, simmer briefly until the sauce is smooth. Taste for seasoning and pour into a heated sauceboat. Cut away the strings from the loin, then carve the meat into 1-inch slices. Each slice of meat will surround a portion of the stuffing. Pass the sauce separately.

NOTE: An alternative method of stuffing the loin is somewhat more demanding but presents a more symmetrical appearance when the meat is sliced. Ask your butcher to tie the loin securely at 1-inch intervals. With a sharp knife make a hole in each end of the loin. Force a long skewer or steel knife sharpener through the length of the loin, turning it to make a tunnel at least ½ inch in diameter. Then, with your fingers, insert the apples and the prunes alternately into the tunnel. Push them through from both sides using a round instrument; the long handle of a wooden spoon would be ideal. Complete the preparation of the meat as above.

Kalvefilet med Sur Fløte
SAUTÉED VEAL SCALLOPS IN SOUR-CREAM SAUCE (NORWEGIAN)

To serve 2 to 4

3 tablespoons unsalted butter	Salt
3 tablespoons vegetable oil	Freshly ground black pepper
¼ cup finely chopped onion	1 cup sour cream
4 large veal scallops, sliced ⅜ inch thick and pounded to a thickness of ¼ inch	½ cup shredded Gjetöst (Norwegian goat cheese)

Heat 1 tablespoon of butter and 1 tablespoon of oil in a heavy 10- to 12-inch skillet over moderate heat. When the foam subsides, add the onions and cook for 3 to 5 minutes, or until they are transparent. With a rubber spatula, scrape them out of the pan into a small bowl and set them aside. Add the remaining butter and oil to the skillet and when the foam subsides, add the veal scallops. Fry them over moderate heat until they are a light golden brown—4 to 5 minutes on each side. Remove them to a heated platter and keep them warm in a 220° oven while you make the sauce.

Pour off all but a thin film of fat from the skillet and add the cooked onions to the pan. Cook over high heat, stirring constantly, for 2 to 5 minutes. Then lower the heat and stir in the sour cream and cheese a little at a time. Continue stirring until the cheese has melted and the sauce is smooth; do not allow it to come to a boil. Taste for seasoning and return the veal to the skillet. Baste the meat with the sauce and let it simmer un-covered for 1 or 2 minutes. Serve immediately.

Små Köttbullar

SMALL SWEDISH MEATBALLS

To serve 6 to 8 (about 50 meatballs)

1 tablespoon butter	1 egg
4 tablespoons finely chopped onion	1 tablespoon finely chopped fresh
1 large boiled potato, mashed (1 cup)	parsley (optional)
3 tablespoons fine dry bread crumbs	2 tablespoons butter
1 pound lean ground beef	2 tablespoons vegetable oil
⅓ cup heavy cream	1 tablespoon flour
1 teaspoon salt	¾ cup light or heavy cream

In a small frying pan, melt the tablespoon of butter over moderate heat. When the foam subsides, add the onions and cook for about 5 minutes, until they are soft and translucent but not brown.

In a large bowl, combine the onions, mashed potato, bread crumbs, meat, cream, salt, egg and optional parsley. Knead vigorously with both hands or beat with a wooden spoon until all of the ingredients are well blended and the mixture is smooth and fluffy. Shape into small balls about 1 inch in diameter. Arrange the meatballs in one layer on a baking sheet or a flat tray, cover them with plastic wrap and chill for at least 1 hour before cooking.

Over high heat, melt the 2 tablespoons of butter and 2 tablespoons of oil in a heavy 10- to 12-inch skillet. When the foam subsides, add the meatballs, 8 to 10 at a time. Reduce the heat to moderate and fry the balls on all sides, shaking the pan almost constantly to roll the balls around in the hot fat to help keep their shape. In 8 to 10 minutes the meatballs should be brown outside and show no trace of pink inside when one is broken open with a knife. Add more butter and oil as needed, and transfer each finished batch to a casserole or baking dish and keep warm in a 200° oven.

If the meatballs are to be served as a main course with noodles or potatoes, you may want to make a sauce with the pan juice. Remove from the heat, pour off all but a thin film of fat from the pan, and stir in 1 tablespoon of flour. Quickly stir in ¾ cup of light or heavy cream, scraping up any browned bits clinging to the pan. Boil the sauce over moderate heat for 2 or 3 minutes, stirring constantly, until it is thick and smooth. Pour over the meatballs and serve.

If the meatballs are to be served as an hors d'oeuvre or as part of a *smörgåsbord,* they should be cooked as above, but formed into smaller balls and served without the sauce.

Lökdolmar
STUFFED ONION ROLLS (SWEDISH)

To serve 4 to 6

½ Swedish meatball recipe *(opposite)*
3 large yellow onions (½ pound each), peeled

3 tablespoons butter
2 tablespoons fresh bread crumbs

Place the peeled onions in a 2- to 3-quart pot, add enough cold water to cover, and bring to a boil over moderate heat. Lower the heat and simmer the onions, uncovered, for 40 minutes. Remove the onions from the pot with a slotted spoon, drain them and let them cool on a platter while you make the meat stuffing *(opposite)*.

Pull off each onion layer separately. They should slide off quite easily. Cut the largest outer layers of the onions in half, but remember to leave them large enough to enclose the stuffing. Discard the inner part of the onions (or use them for some other purpose) if the leaves are too small to stuff. Put a heaping teaspoon of the meat stuffing in the middle of each onion leaf and enclose it by folding over the edges of the leaf. (At this point they may be covered with plastic wrap and refrigerated for up to 2 days before cooking.)

Preheat the oven to 400°. In a shallow 1- to 1½-quart flameproof baking dish, melt 3 tablespoons of butter over low heat. Remove the dish from the heat and place the onion rolls, sealed side down, side by side in the butter, first rolling each in the butter to coat it. Bake 15 minutes, then baste with the butter in the dish, sprinkle with the bread crumbs, and bake another 15 minutes, until the onions are lightly browned and the crumbs crisp. *Lökdolmar* may be served as part of a *smörgåsbord*, or as a main dish.

Färsrulader

STUFFED VEAL ROULADES (SWEDISH)

Makes 16 roulades (to serve 4 to 6)

2 cups cold water
1 medium boiling potato, peeled and
  quartered
2 tablespoons butter
¼ cup finely chopped onions
1 pound finely ground veal
3 tablespoons fine dry bread crumbs
⅓ cup heavy cream
2 tablespoons water

1½ teaspoons salt
½ teaspoon white pepper
1 egg
2 tablespoons finely chopped parsley
1 tablespoon cornstarch
½ cup paper-thin slices of leeks,
  white part only
8 tablespoons (1 quarter-pound stick)
  butter
¼ cup heavy cream

In a 1- to 1½-quart saucepan, bring the water to a boil. Add the quartered potato and boil 10 to 15 minutes, or until tender. Drain and mash with a fork. In a small frying pan, melt 2 tablespoons of butter. When the foam subsides, add the chopped onions and cook 7 or 8 minutes, stirring frequently, until they are soft and transparent but not brown. Scrape the onions into a large mixing bowl, and add the mashed potato, ground veal, bread crumbs, cream, water, salt, pepper, egg, parsley and cornstarch. Mix well, then refrigerate at least 1 hour. Brush a large wooden pastry board (or another hard, smooth surface) with water and pat or roll out the mixture to a 16-by-16-inch square about ⅛ inch thick. Your hands or the rolling pin should be moistened with water to prevent the ground-meat mixture from sticking. With a pastry wheel or small, sharp knife, cut the rectangle of meat into 16 squares of 4 by 4 inches each. Put a thin layer of leek slices (about 1½ teaspoons) on each square. Now with the aid of a knife or, better still, an icing spatula, roll up each square, jelly-roll fashion. Ideally, they should now be chilled, but they may, if necessary, be cooked immediately.

Heat 2 tablespoons of butter in a heavy 10- to 12-inch skillet. When the foam subsides, add the roulades, 4 at a time, turning them gently with a spatula so that they brown on all sides. When they are a rich brown, set them aside on a heated platter in a 200° oven. Repeat the process, adding 2 tablespoons of fresh butter for every 4 roulades. Pour the ¼ cup of heavy cream into the empty pan and boil it rapidly for 3 to 5 minutes, until it thickens, meanwhile scraping up the browned bits in the pan with a rubber spatula or a wooden spoon. Taste for seasoning, add salt if needed, and pour over the waiting roulades. If you must, cover the platter with aluminum foil and keep warm in a 200° oven for not more than 15 minutes.

Pikanta Oxrulader

ROULADES OF BEEF STUFFED WITH ANCHOVIES AND ONIONS (SWEDISH)

To serve 4

2 pounds top round steak
Salt
Freshly ground black pepper
4 tablespoons butter

4 tablespoons vegetable oil
1 cup finely chopped onions
2 tablespoons flour
16 flat anchovy fillets, washed and
   dried
½ cup water

Ask the butcher to cut the meat in 8 slices, each approximately ⅜ inch thick, 6 inches long and 3 inches wide, and to pound them to ⅛ inch thick, or cut and pound it yourself between 2 pieces of wax paper with a meat pounder or the flat of a cleaver.

Heat 1 tablespoon of the butter with 2 tablespoons of the oil in a small skillet and in it sauté the chopped onions for 5 to 8 minutes, or until they are tender and golden. Remove from the heat and stir in the flour. Now return to low heat and cook for 1 to 2 minutes, stirring constantly. Reserve 2 tablespoons of this *roux* for the sauce. Sprinkle each slice of meat liberally with salt and a few grindings of pepper, and spread the remainder of the *roux* evenly over each slice of meat. Lay 2 anchovy fillets on each slice, roll them up securely and either tie with a loop of cord at each end or fasten with a wooden toothpick inserted through the roll lengthwise.

Heat the remaining 3 tablespoons of butter and 2 tablespoons of oil in a heavy 10- to 12-inch sauté pan over moderate heat. When the foam subsides, add the roulades, 4 at a time. Turn the roulades with kitchen tongs to brown them on all sides. Arrange the browned roulades in a single layer in a 2- to 2½-quart casserole or baking dish that is equipped with a cover. The preparation of the roulades may be done in advance up to this point.

Preheat the oven to 350°. Deglaze the pan by pouring in the ½ cup of water and boiling for 1 or 2 minutes, stirring to scrape up any bits clinging to the pan. Add the reserved *roux* and cook over medium-high heat for 2 or 3 more minutes, stirring briskly, until the sauce has thickened. Pour over the roulades, cover and bake for 45 minutes. Serve the *oxrulader* with mashed potatoes and gherkins or relish.

Biff à la Lindström

HAMBURGERS À LA LINDSTRÖM (SWEDISH)

To serve 4 to 6

1 tablespoon butter
2 tablespoons finely chopped onions
1 pound lean ground beef
4 egg yolks
1 tablespoon capers, drained and
   finely chopped
1½ teaspoons salt

Freshly ground black pepper
2 teaspoons white vinegar
½ cup heavy cream
¼ cup finely chopped drained beets,
   freshly cooked or canned
2 tablespoons butter
2 tablespoons vegetable oil
4 to 6 fried eggs (optional)

In a small pan, melt the 1 tablespoon of butter. When the foam subsides, add the onions and cook for 2 or 3 minutes, or until they are soft and transparent but not brown. Scrape into a large bowl, and add the meat, egg yolks, capers, salt, a few grindings of pepper and white vinegar. Mix together and moisten with the heavy cream. Then stir in the drained chopped beets. Shape the mixture into 12 to 14 round patties, about 2 to 3 inches in diameter. In a heavy, large skillet, heat the butter and oil. When the foam subsides, add the patties, 3 or 4 at a time, and cook over moderately high heat for 5 to 6 minutes on each side, or until they are a deep brown. In Sweden, these spicy hamburgers are frequently served with a fried egg set atop each, in which case they are made larger and thicker.

Flaeskesteg med Svaer

ROAST FRESH HAM WITH CRACKLING (DANISH)

To serve 8 to 10

½ fresh ham (butt or shank) weighing
   about 6 pounds or 6 pounds

shoulder of pork with the rind on
Coarse salt or substitute regular salt
Freshly ground black pepper

Preheat the oven to 300°. Using a sharp, heavy knife, cut deeply through the rind and fat until you reach the meat, making the incisions ½ inch apart lengthwise and crosswise. Rub salt and pepper liberally into these gashes. Insert a meat thermometer into the thickest part of the ham and place it on a rack set in a shallow roasting pan just large enough to hold the meat comfortably. Roast slowly 4 to 4½ hours, or until the meat thermometer reads 180°. Do not baste the meat. When roasted, the meat should be moist and tender, and the rind (or crackling) very crisp. Let the roast rest outside the oven for 10 to 15 minutes for easier carving. A little of the crackling should be included in each serving of meat.

Frikadeller

DANISH MEAT PATTIES

Makes 8 to 10 patties

½ pound boneless veal
½ pound boneless pork
1 medium onion, coarsely chopped or grated (½ cup)
3 tablespoons flour

1½ cups club soda
1 egg, well beaten
1 teaspoon salt
¼ teaspoon pepper
4 tablespoons butter
2 tablespoons vegetable oil

Put the veal, pork and chopped onion twice through the finest blade of a meat grinder, or have the butcher grind the meats together and then grate in the onion yourself.

In a large mixing bowl, vigorously beat the flour into the ground meat mixture with a wooden spoon, or use an electric mixer equipped with a pastry arm or paddle. Gradually beat in the club soda, a few tablespoons at a time, and continue to beat until the meat is light and fluffy. Now thoroughly beat in the egg, salt and pepper. Cover the bowl with aluminum foil or plastic wrap and refrigerate for 1 hour; this will make the meat mixture firmer and easier to handle.

Shape the mixture into oblongs about 4 inches long, 2 inches wide and 1 inch thick. Melt the butter and oil over high heat in a heavy 10- to 12-inch skillet. When the foam subsides, lower the heat to moderate and add the meat patties, 4 or 5 at a time, taking care not to crowd them. Cook about 6 to 8 minutes on each side, turning the patties with a wide spatula or two wooden spoons. When they are a rich mahogany brown, remove them from the pan and set them aside on a heated platter. Continue with the remaining patties. Because *frikadeller* contain pork, they should never be served rare. To be certain they are cooked through, puncture one with the tip of a small knife. The juices should run clear and show no tinge of pink.

Frikadeller are traditionally accompanied by boiled potatoes and pickled beets *(page 48)*, cucumber salad *(page 48)* or red cabbage *(page 51)*.

Dillkött på Lamm

LAMB IN DILL SAUCE (SWEDISH)

To serve 6 to 8

4 pounds breast or shoulder of lamb,
   cut in 2-inch cubes
4 to 5 cups water

Bouquet of 1 bay leaf, 5 sprigs
   dill and 5 sprigs parsley, tied
   together with a string
1 tablespoon salt
4 whole peppercorns, white if possible

In a heavy 4- to 6-quart casserole that is equipped with a cover, cover the lamb with 4 to 5 cups of cold water and bring it to a boil, uncovered, over high heat. Lower the heat to moderate and with a large spoon skim off and discard the scum as it rises to the surface. Add the bouquet and the salt and peppercorns to the pot. Partially cover the pot and simmer the lamb very slowly for about 1½ hours, or until the meat is tender when pierced with the tip of a sharp knife. With a slotted spoon, remove the lamb to a deep heated platter or casserole, cover with foil and keep warm in a 200° oven.

DILL SAUCE

2 tablespoons butter
2 tablespoons flour
2½ cups reduced lamb stock
   (from above)
3 tablespoons chopped fresh dill
1 tablespoon white vinegar

2 teaspoons sugar
½ teaspoon salt
½ teaspoon lemon juice
1 egg yolk, lightly beaten
Dill sprigs
Lemon slices

To make the sauce, strain the lamb stock from the casserole through a fine sieve into a 1½- to 2-quart shallow saucepan and boil it down rapidly over high heat until it is reduced to 2½ cups. Meanwhile, in another 1-quart saucepan, melt the 2 tablespoons of butter. Remove this pan from the heat, stir in the 2 tablespoons of flour, then add all of the reduced lamb stock at once, stirring it rapidly with a wire whisk. Return the pan to the heat and bring the sauce to a boil, whisking constantly, until it is smooth and thick. Simmer the sauce over low heat for about 5 minutes, stirring frequently. Add the chopped dill, vinegar, sugar, salt and lemon juice. Stir a couple of tablespoons of the hot sauce into the beaten egg yolk, then pour this mixture slowly back into the sauce, beating constantly with a wire whisk. Heat through again, but do not let the sauce boil. Taste for seasoning, add salt and pepper if necessary, and strain the sauce through a fine sieve over the lamb. Garnish the platter with additional sprigs of dill and lemon slices, and serve with boiled buttered new potatoes or rice.

Får i kål

LAMB-AND-CABBAGE CASSEROLE (NORWEGIAN)

To serve 6

2 tablespoons vegetable oil

3½ pounds breast of lamb, well trimmed of fat and cut into 2-inch cubes

⅓ cup flour

1½- to 2-pound white cabbage, washed, cored and sliced into 1-inch wedges

1 cup diced celery

1½ cups sliced onions

2 tablespoons salt

2½ cups beef or chicken stock, fresh or canned

2 tablespoons whole black peppercorns, tied in cheesecloth and lightly bruised with a rolling pin or pestle

Preheat the oven to 350°. Heat the oil in a heavy 10- to 12-inch skillet over high heat until a light haze forms over it. Add the cubed meat and cook over medium-high heat, turning the cubes with a wooden spoon until they are evenly browned. Using tongs, transfer the meat to a large mixing bowl. Sprinkle it with the flour and toss lightly with a wooden spoon until the meat cubes are evenly coated and no trace of flour remains. Set the skillet aside.

In a 5- to 6-quart casserole equipped with a cover, arrange a layer of the browned meat and another of cabbage wedges. Sprinkle with half of the celery and half of the onions, and salt each layer lightly. Repeat, ending with a layer of cabbage. Now deglaze the skillet in which you browned the meat by first pouring off nearly all of the fat, leaving only a thin film on the bottom of the pan. Then pour in the stock, stir vigorously over high heat with a wooden spoon and scrape up any browned bits clinging to the bottom or sides of the pan. Pour the liquid over the meat and cabbage in the casserole. Add the bag of peppercorns, cover the casserole and bake for 1½ hours, or until the meat is tender when pierced with the tip of a sharp knife.

Pytt i Panna

SWEDISH HASH

To serve 4 to 6

5 to 6 medium potatoes, peeled and
    diced into ¼-inch pieces (4 cups)
1 pound roast or boiled beef or lamb,
    diced into ¼-inch pieces (2 cups)
½ pound smoked or boiled ham,
    diced into ¼-inch pieces (1 cup)

2 tablespoons butter
2 tablespoons oil
2 medium yellow onions, finely
    chopped (about 1 cup)
1 tablespoon finely chopped parsley
Salt
Freshly ground black pepper
4 to 6 fried eggs or 4 to 6 raw egg yolks

The ingredients in *pytt i panna,* unlike those in most hashes, are cooked separately to retain their individual character. To present this dish in its most attractive and traditional form, it is essential that the potatoes and meat be diced into small pieces as neatly and uniformly as possible. Peel the potatoes and cut them in half lengthwise. Place them flat side down and cut them lengthwise into ¼-inch strips. Then cut these strips crosswise into ¼-inch strips. Drop the resulting dice into cold water to prevent them from discoloring. When ready to use, drain them in a colander, spread them out in a single layer on paper towels, and pat them thoroughly dry with more towels. Similarly cut the meats into ¼-inch dice.

    Melt the butter and oil in a heavy 10- to 12-inch skillet over high heat. When the foam subsides, add the potatoes. Lower the heat to moderate and fry the potatoes for about 15 to 20 minutes, turning them about in the pan with a spoon until they are crisp and golden. Remove them from the pan and set them aside to drain on a double thickness of paper towels. Add a little more butter and oil to the pan if necessary, and in it, cook the onions until they are soft and transparent but not brown. Add the diced meats, raise the heat slightly, and fry with the onions about another 10 minutes. Shake the pan often so that the meat cubes brown lightly on all sides. Stir the fried potatoes into the meat and onions and cook briefly to heat the potatoes thoroughly. Then sprinkle the hash with parsley. Add salt and freshly ground black pepper to taste.

    Arrange individual servings of the hash on warm plates. Make a depression in each serving with the back of a large spoon and top with a fried egg. Or you may wish to serve the hash in the traditional Swedish way: to do this, place a raw egg yolk in half of an eggshell and nestle the eggshell into each serving. The diners themselves mix the raw yolk into the hot hash.

Hökarepanna

COACHMAN'S PAN (SWEDISH)

To serve 4 to 6

2 pounds boiling potatoes
2 tablespoons butter
2 tablespoons vegetable oil
3 medium onions, thinly sliced
4 lamb kidneys, or 1 veal or 2 pork
    kidneys

¾ pound boneless pork loin, in ¼-
    inch-thick slices
1½ cups beer
1½ cups beef stock, fresh or canned
½ teaspoon sugar
Salt
Freshly ground black pepper
1 bay leaf

Preheat the oven to 350°. Peel the potatoes and slice them ⅛ inch thick; set them aside in a bowl of cold water to prevent discoloration.

Heat the butter and oil in a heavy 10- to 12-inch skillet over moderately high heat. When the foam subsides, add the onions and cook them until they are soft and lightly colored. Remove them to a dish with a slotted spoon. Add more butter and oil to the skillet if necessary, and in it brown the kidneys and pork slices quickly, turning with tongs several times to brown them evenly. Remove the meats from the skillet and slice the kidneys ¼ inch thick. Now deglaze the pan by adding the beer, stock and sugar and boiling them over high heat for 2 or 3 minutes, meanwhile scraping into the liquid any browned bits of onions or meat clinging to the bottom and sides of the pan. Remove the pan from the heat and set aside.

Drain the potatoes and pat them dry with paper towels. Arrange 2 or 3 layers of potatoes, meat and onions alternately in a 3-quart oven-to-table casserole, finishing with a layer of potatoes on top. Season each layer with salt and pepper as you proceed, and place the bay leaf in the center of the top layer. Pour in the deglazing liquid; it should just cover the top layer in the casserole. Add more stock if it does not.

Bring the casserole to a boil on top of the stove and then bake, uncovered, in the center of the oven for about 1 hour and 40 minutes, or until the top potato layer is brown and tender when pierced with the tip of a sharp knife.

Serve directly from the casserole as a one-dish meal.

Lihamurekepiiras

MEAT LOAF IN SOUR-CREAM PASTRY (FINNISH)

To serve 6 to 8

PASTRY
2¼ cups flour
1 teaspoon salt

12 tablespoons chilled unsalted butter,
cut into ¼-inch bits
1 egg
½ cup sour cream
1 tablespoon soft butter

SOUR CREAM PASTRY: Sift the flour and salt together into a large chilled bowl. Drop the ¼-inch bits of butter into the bowl. Working quickly, use your fingertips to rub the flour and butter together until they have the appearance of flakes of coarse meal. In a separate bowl, mix together the egg and sour cream and stir into this the flour-butter mixture, working with your fingers until you can gather the dough into a soft, pliable ball. Wrap in wax paper and refrigerate 1 hour. Cut the chilled dough in half and roll out each half to rectangles of 6 by 14 inches each, setting aside any scraps.

Butter the bottom of a jelly-roll pan with 1 tablespoon of soft butter. Lift 1 sheet of the pastry over the rolling pin and unroll it into the pan, or drape the pastry over the rolling pin, lift it up and unfold it into the pan.

MEAT FILLING

4 tablespoons butter
¾ cup finely chopped mushrooms
(about ¼ pound fresh mushrooms)
3 pounds finely ground meat (beef,
pork, ham, lamb or veal or a
combination of any of these), or
4 cups cooked ground or finely

chopped meat
2 tablespoons all-purpose flour
⅓ cup finely chopped onions
¼ cup finely chopped parsley
1 cup freshly grated Cheddar, Swiss
or Gruyère cheese
½ cup milk
1 egg combined with 2 tablespoons
milk

MEAT FILLING: Melt the butter in a 10- to 12-inch skillet. When the foam subsides, add the mushrooms and cook over moderate heat, stirring frequently, for 6 to 8 minutes, or until they are lightly colored. If you are using raw meat, add it to the skillet and cook, stirring occasionally, for another 8 to 10 minutes, or until the meat loses its red color and any liquid in the pan evaporates. Stir in the flour. Scrape the meat mixture from the skillet (or the mushrooms and already cooked meat) into a large mixing bowl and stir in the chopped onions, parsley, cheese and milk. Gather this meat mixture into a ball and place it in the center of the dough in the pan. With your hands, pat the meat into a narrow loaf extending lengthwise down the center of the dough from one end to the other. Lift the second sheet of pastry over the pin and gently drape it on top of the meat loaf; press the edges of the 2 sheets together. Dip a pastry brush into the combined egg-and-milk mixture and moisten the edges of the dough. Press down on the edges all around the loaf with the back of a fork (the tines will seal the edges securely). Prick the top of the loaf in several places with a fork to allow steam to escape.

Preheat the oven to 375°. Gather together into a ball all of the excess scraps of dough and roll it out to a thin rectangle. With a pastry wheel or small, sharp knife, cut this dough into long, narrow strips. Brush the loaf with more of the egg and milk mixture and crisscross the pastry strips over the top of the loaf in an attractive pattern. Now brush the strips with the milk and egg mixture and set the jelly-roll pan in the center of the oven. Bake for 45 minutes, or until the loaf has turned a golden brown. Serve thick slices of the hot meat loaf, accompanied by a bowl of cold sour cream and a side dish of lingonberries.

Kalops

BEEF STEW WITH SOUR CREAM (SWEDISH)

To serve 4

2 tablespoons butter	½ teaspoon salt
2 tablespoons vegetable oil	¼ teaspoon ground allspice
2 pounds boneless beef chuck, cut in	⅛ teaspoon freshly ground black
1½-inch cubes	pepper
1 large onion, thinly sliced	1 bay leaf
1 tablespoon flour	1¼ cups beef stock, freshly made
	or canned
	2 tablespoons sour cream

Preheat the oven to 350°. Heat the butter and oil in a heavy 10- to 12-inch skillet. When the foam subsides, add the meat and brown it well on all sides. Transfer the meat to a 3- to 4-quart casserole equipped with a cover. Add the sliced onion to the skillet (with more butter and oil if necessary) and cook over moderate heat until soft and transparent. Scrape them into the casserole, add the flour and toss the ingredients lightly with a wooden spoon to coat them evenly. Add the salt, allspice, pepper and bay leaf. Pour the stock into the skillet and boil it rapidly for 2 or 3 minutes, scraping into the liquid any browned bits of meat and onions clinging to the pan. Pour into the casserole. Bring the casserole to a boil on top of the stove, cover it tightly, then set in the lower third of the oven. Cook, lowering the oven heat if necessary, so that the sauce in the casserole barely simmers. In about 1¼ hours, the meat should be tender when pierced with the tip of a sharp knife. Remove the meat to a deep, heated platter and cover it lightly with foil. With a large spoon, skim the fat from the liquid in the casserole and discard it. With a wire whisk, beat in the sour cream, a tablespoon at a time. Taste and season with salt and pepper, and reheat if necessary. Then pour the finished sauce over the meat.

Slottsstek

ROYAL POT ROAST (SWEDISH)

To serve 6 to 8

2 tablespoons butter
2 tablespoons vegetable oil
4 pounds boneless beef: bottom
round, rump, brisket or chuck roast
1 cup finely chopped onions
3 tablespoons flour
1 tablespoon dark corn syrup

2 tablespoons white vinegar
2 cups beef stock, fresh or canned
1 large bay leaf
6 flat anchovy fillets, washed and dried
1 teaspoon whole peppercorns, crushed
and tied in cheesecloth
Freshly ground black pepper
Salt

Preheat the oven to 350°. In a heavy 5- to 6-quart casserole equipped with a cover, melt the butter and oil over moderate heat. When the foam subsides, add the meat and brown it on all sides; this should take at least 15 minutes. Remove the meat from the pan and set it aside. Add the chopped onions to the casserole and let them cook over moderately high heat for 6 to 8 minutes, stirring occasionally, until they are lightly browned. Remove the pan from the heat and add the flour. Stir gently to dissolve it, and pour in the dark corn syrup, white vinegar and 2 cups of stock. Add the bay leaf, anchovies and bag of peppercorns, replace the meat in the casserole, cover and bring to a boil on top of the stove. Place the casserole in the lower third of the oven, regulating the heat so that the liquid in the casserole barely simmers. The meat should be tender in about 3 hours. To test, pierce it with the tip of a sharp knife; the roast should offer no resistance.

Transfer the pot roast to a heated platter and cover it lightly with foil to keep it warm. Remove the bay leaf and bag of peppercorns from the casserole and discard them. Skim off any surface fat and taste the remaining sauce; add salt and pepper if necessary. If the sauce seems to lack flavor, boil it briskly, uncovered, over high heat for a few minutes to reduce and concentrate it. Pour into a heated sauceboat and serve with the meat. In Sweden slottsstek is usually accompanied by red currant jelly or lingonberries, and often with gherkins and boiled potatoes.

Maksalaatikko

LIVER-AND-RICE CASSEROLE (FINNISH)

To serve 6 to 8

4 quarts boiling salted water
1 cup white
   long-grain rice
2 tablespoons butter
1 medium onion, finely chopped
   (⅓ cup)
2 cups milk
2 eggs, lightly beaten

¼ cup cooked and crumbled lean
   bacon (about 4 slices)
½ cup raisins
2 tablespoons dark corn syrup
2 teaspoons salt
¼ teaspoon white pepper
¼ teaspoon ground marjoram
1½ pounds calf or beef liver, finely
   ground
1 tablespoon butter

Cook the rice in 4 quarts of briskly boiling salted water for about 12 minutes. When the rice is still slightly firm when tasted, drain it thoroughly in a colander and set it aside.

In a heavy 6- to 8-inch frying pan, melt the 2 tablespoons of butter over moderate heat. When the foam subsides, add the onions and cook them for 3 to 5 minutes, or until they are soft and transparent but not brown. Remove from the heat and set aside.

Preheat the oven to 350°. In a large mixing bowl, gently combine the approximately 3 cups of cooked rice, milk and lightly beaten eggs. Add the cooked onions, crumbled bacon, raisins and corn syrup, and season with the salt, pepper and marjoram. Stir in the ground liver and mix thoroughly.

With a pastry brush or paper towels, spread a 2-quart casserole or baking dish with the tablespoon of butter and pour in the liver-rice mixture. Bake uncovered in the middle of the oven for 1 to 1½ hours, or until a knife inserted in the center of the casserole comes out clean. Serve hot, accompanied by lingonberries or cranberry sauce.

Sauces

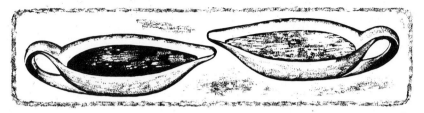

Tomatsmør
TOMATO BUTTER (NORWEGIAN)

To make ½ cup

8 tablespoons (1 quarter-pound stick) unsalted butter

2 tablespoons tomato paste
½ teaspoon salt
¼ teaspoon sugar

Cream the butter with an electric mixer set at medium speed or by beating it against the side of a bowl with a wooden spoon. When it is light and fluffy, beat in the tomato paste, salt and sugar. Transfer to a serving bowl and chill until ready to serve. Serve cold, with hot grilled or fried fish.

Pepperrotsmør
HORSE-RADISH BUTTER (NORWEGIAN)

To make ½ cup

8 tablespoons (1 quarter-pound stick) unsalted butter

2 tablespoons freshly grated horse-radish root or 2 tablespoons bottled prepared horse-radish
¼ teaspoon salt

Cream the butter with an electric mixer set at medium speed or by beating it against the side of a bowl with a wooden spoon until it is light and fluffy. If you are using prepared horse-radish, drain it and squeeze it dry in a kitchen towel or double thickness of cheesecloth. Now beat the horse-radish and the salt into the creamed butter. Transfer the horse-radish butter to a small serving dish and chill until you are ready to use it. Serve cold, with hot grilled or fried fish.

Persillesovs
PARSLEY SAUCE (DANISH)

To make about 1½ cups

2 tablespoons unsalted butter
2 tablespoons flour
1 cup chicken stock,

freshly made or canned
Salt
2 tablespoons finely chopped parsley
2 teaspoons lemon juice

In a small, heavy saucepan, melt the butter over moderate heat. When the foam subsides, remove from the heat and stir in the flour with a wooden spoon. Pour in the stock all at once, beating vigorously with a wire whisk until the butter and flour *roux* and the liquid are well-blended. Return to low heat and cook, whisking constantly, until the sauce comes to a boil and is smooth and thick. Reduce the heat and simmer slowly for 2 to 3 minutes. Add salt to taste, stir in the parsley and lemon juice, and pour the sauce over fish fillets *(page 19)*.

Rekesaus
SHRIMP SAUCE (NORWEGIAN)

To make about 2 cups

4 tablespoons butter
4 tablespoons flour
2 cups milk
¼ cup heavy cream

1½ teaspoons salt
¼ teaspoon white pepper
1½ tablespoons lemon juice
1 to 2 pounds medium shrimp, cooked
    and finely chopped
2 tablespoons finely chopped fresh dill

In a 1½- to 2-quart enameled or stainless-steel saucepan, melt the butter over moderate heat. Remove from the heat and stir in the flour. Pour in the milk and cream all at once and, stirring constantly with a wire whisk, place over low heat and cook until the sauce is smooth and thick. Season with salt, pepper and lemon juice, then add the chopped cooked shrimp and cook another 1 or 2 minutes, until the shrimp are heated through. Stir in the dill and serve with hot fish pudding *(page 20)* or boiled fish. Cooked cauliflower, served with this sauce, is a very popular luncheon dish.

Gravlaxsås

MUSTARD-AND-DILL SAUCE (SWEDISH)

To make about ¾ cup

4 tablespoons dark, highly seasoned
   prepared mustard
1 teaspoon powdered mustard

3 tablespoons sugar
2 tablespoons white vinegar
⅓ cup vegetable oil
3 tablespoons fresh chopped dill

In a small, deep bowl, mix the two mustards, sugar and vinegar to a paste. With a wire whisk, slowly beat in the oil until it forms a thick mayonnaise-like emulsion. Stir in the dill. The sauce may be kept refrigerated in a tightly covered jar for several days, but will need to be shaken vigorously or beaten with a whisk to remix the ingredients before serving with *gravlax (page 15)* or other cold seafood.

Vaniljsås

COLD VANILLA SAUCE (SWEDISH)

To make about 1½ cups

¼ cup sugar
1 tablespoon cornstarch

¼ teaspoon salt
2 egg yolks
2 cups light cream
1 teaspoon vanilla

Mix the sugar, cornstarch and salt together in a heavy 1½- to 2-quart stainless-steel or enameled saucepan. Beat the egg yolks and cream together in a bowl and pour slowly into the sugar, cornstarch and salt in the saucepan, beating constantly with a wire whisk. Continue to whisk over low heat until the sauce is smooth and thick, but do not let it boil. Remove the pan from the heat and stir in the vanilla. Immediately transfer the sauce to a bowl, cool, then cover with plastic wrap and chill.

Serve the cold sauce in a sauceboat with apple cake *(page 62)* or other suitable desserts. Or, spoon a little sauce over each serving of the dessert before presenting it at the table.

Vegetables and Garnishes

Halve Aebler med Svedsker

POACHED APPLE HALVES STUFFED WITH PRUNES IN PORT WINE (DANISH)

To serve 8

16 medium prunes
2 teaspoons sugar

⅔ cup port wine
8 baking apples, ½ pound each
1 cup sugar
1 quart cold water

In an enameled, stainless-steel or ovenproof glass bowl, combine the wine, sugar and prunes. Marinate the prunes in this mixture for at least 6 hours, then preheat the oven to 350°. Bake the prunes in their bowl, uncovered, for about 30 minutes, or until they are tender but not falling apart.

Meanwhile, prepare the poached apples. Pare the apples and cut them in half vertically. Scoop out the cores as neatly as possible with a small, sharp knife. In a 2- to 3-quart enameled or stainless-steel saucepan, combine the sugar and water, bring to a boil, and boil steadily for 2 or 3 minutes. Then lower the heat and add the apple halves, 8 at a time. Simmer for 10 minutes, until they are tender but not too soft. Transfer the poached apples to a heated platter with a slotted spoon and poach the remaining apples. Drain the baked prunes of all of their liquid and place 1 prune in each apple half.

To prepare these in advance, cover with plastic wrap and refrigerate. Just before serving, place the prune-filled apples on a lightly buttered cookie sheet, cover with foil and bake 10 minutes in a preheated 400° oven. Serve with roast goose *(page 24)*, or duck, as part of the traditional Danish Christmas dinner.

Syltede Rødbeder
PICKLED BEETS (DANISH)

Makes 2 cups

½ cup white vinegar
½ cup water
½ cup sugar

1 teaspoon salt
⅛ teaspoon freshly ground black
    pepper
2 cups thinly sliced freshly cooked or
    canned beets

In a stainless-steel or enameled 1½- to 2-quart saucepan, combine the vinegar, water, sugar, salt and pepper, bring to a boil and boil briskly for 2 minutes. Meanwhile, place the sliced beets in a deep glass, stainless-steel or enamel bowl. Pour the hot marinade over the beets and let them cool uncovered to room temperature. Cover the bowl with plastic wrap and refrigerate for at least 12 hours, stirring every few hours to keep the slices moist.

Agurkesalat
PICKLED CUCUMBER SALAD (DANISH)

To serve 4

2 large (8-inch) or 3 medium (6-inch)
    cucumbers
1 tablespoon salt

¾ cup white vinegar
1 tablespoon sugar
1 teaspoon salt
¼ teaspoon white pepper
2 tablespoons chopped fresh dill

Scrub the wax coating (if any) off the cucumbers and dry them. Score the cucumbers lengthwise with a fork and cut them in the thinnest possible slices; ideally, the slices should be almost translucent. Arrange them in a thin layer in a shallow china or glass dish and sprinkle with salt. Place 2 or 3 plates on top of the cucumbers (to press out excess water and bitterness) and let them rest at room temperature for a couple of hours.

Remove the plates, drain the cucumbers of all their liquid, and spread them out on paper towels. Gently pat the cucumbers dry with paper towels and return them to their dish. In a small bowl, beat together the vinegar, sugar, salt and pepper. Pour over the cucumbers and strew them with the chopped dill. Chill for 2 or 3 hours and just before serving, drain away nearly all of the liquid. Serve as a salad, as a garnish on different smørrebrød, or with meat and poultry.

FREE RESERVATION NUMBER
800-547-8010
*In Oregon, please call your nearest
Thunderbird or Red Lion Motor Inn or Motel.

RED LION MOTOR INN

Brunede Kartofler
CARAMELIZED POTATOES (DANISH)

To serve 8

24 small new potatoes

½ cup sugar
8 tablespoons (1 quarter-pound stick)
  unsalted butter, melted

Drop the unpeeled potatoes into a pan of boiling water and cook 15 to 20 minutes, or until they offer no resistance when pierced with the tip of a sharp knife. Let them cool slightly; then peel them.

Melt the ½ cup of sugar in a heavy 10- to 12-inch skillet over low heat. Cook slowly for 3 to 5 minutes, until the sugar turns to a light-brown caramel. Stir constantly with a wooden spoon and watch the sugar closely; the syrup changes color very rapidly and burns easily. It must not become too dark or it will be bitter. Stir in the melted butter, and add as many potatoes as possible without crowding the pan. Shake the pan almost constantly to roll the potatoes and coat them on all sides with the caramel. Remove the hot, caramelized potatoes to a heated serving bowl and repeat the procedure until all the potatoes are coated.

Brynt Potatis i Ugn
OVEN-BROWNED POTATO WEDGES (SWEDISH)

To serve 4 to 6

4 medium-sized baking potatoes

4 tablespoons melted butter
Salt

Preheat the oven to 450°. Peel the potatoes and cut them in half lengthwise. Stand each half upright on a chopping board and slice it in thirds down its length, making 3 wedge-shaped pieces. Blanch the wedges by cooking them rapidly for 3 minutes in enough unsalted boiling water to cover them. Drain and pat them dry with paper towels.

With a pastry brush or paper towels, butter a baking dish large enough to hold the potatoes side by side in a single layer. Dribble melted butter over the tops and sprinkle them liberally with salt. Roast them in the center of the oven for 15 minutes, turn them, and roast another 15 minutes.

These crisp potato wedges make excellent accompaniments to roasted meats or poultry.

Smørdampete Nypoteter
BUTTER-STEAMED NEW POTATOES (NORWEGIAN)

To serve 4 to 6

	unsalted butter
20 to 24 tiny new potatoes	1 teaspoon salt
(about 1 inch in diameter)	⅛ teaspoon white pepper
8 tablespoons (1 quarter-pound stick)	3 tablespoons finely chopped fresh dill

Scrub the potatoes under cold running water; then pat them thoroughly dry with paper towels. Melt the ¼ pound of butter in a heavy, 6-quart casserole equipped with a cover. Add the potatoes and sprinkle them with salt and pepper. Then coat them thoroughly with the melted butter by rolling them about in the casserole. To ensure the success of this dish, the cover must fit the casserole tightly; if you have doubts, cover the casserole with a double thickness of aluminum foil, and pinch down the edges to seal it before putting on the lid. Cook over low heat (an asbestos pad under the pan ensures against scorching) for 30 to 45 minutes, depending on the size of the potatoes. Shake the casserole from time to time to prevent the potatoes from sticking. When the potatoes can be easily pierced with the tip of a sharp knife, they are done. Arrange them on a heated serving plate, sprinkle them with the chopped dill, and serve at once.

Hasselbackpotatis
ROASTED POTATOES (SWEDISH)

To serve 6

6 baking potatoes, about 4 inches long	1 teaspoon salt
and 2 inches wide	2 tablespoons dry bread crumbs
1 tablespoon soft butter	2 tablespoons grated imported
3 tablespoons melted butter	Parmesan cheese (optional)

Preheat the oven to 425°. Peel the potatoes and drop them into a bowl of cold water to prevent them from discoloring. Place one potato at a time on a wooden spoon large enough to cradle it comfortably, and beginning at about ½ inch from the end, slice down at ⅛-inch intervals. (The deep, curved bowl of the wooden spoon will prevent the knife from slicing completely through the potato.) Drop each semisliced potato back into the cold water.

When you are ready to roast them, drain the potatoes and pat them dry with paper towels. With a pastry brush or paper towels, generously butter a baking dish large enough to hold the potatoes side by side in one layer and arrange them in it cut side up. Baste the potatoes with 1½ tablespoons of the melted butter, sprinkle them liberally with salt, and set them in the center of the oven. After 30 minutes sprinkle a few of the bread crumbs over the surface of each potato, baste with the remaining melted butter and the butter in the pan, and continue to roast another 15 minutes, or until the potatoes are golden brown and show no resistance when pierced with the tip of a sharp knife. If you wish to use the cheese, it should be strewn over the potatoes 5 minutes before they are done.

Rødkaal

BRAISED RED CABBAGE (DANISH)

To serve 6	1 tablespoon sugar
	1 teaspoon salt
1 medium head red cabbage, 2 to	⅓ cup water
2½ pounds	⅓ cup white vinegar
4 tablespoons butter, cut into small	¼ cup red currant jelly
pieces	2 tablespoons grated apple

Wash the head of cabbage under cold running water, remove the tough outer leaves, and cut the cabbage in half from top to bottom. Lay the flat sides down on the chopping board, cut away the core and slice the cabbage very finely. There should be approximately 9 cups of shredded cabbage when you finish.

Preheat the oven to 325°. Combine the butter, sugar, salt, water and vinegar in a heavy stainless-steel or enameled 4- to 5-quart casserole. When it comes to a boil and the butter has melted, add the shredded cabbage and toss thoroughly with two wooden spoons or forks. Bring to a boil again, cover tightly and place in the center of the oven to braise for 2 hours. There is little danger that the cabbage will dry out during the cooking, but it is a good idea to check on the liquid level occasionally. Add a little water if it seems necessary.

About 10 minutes before the cabbage is finished, stir in the jelly and grated apple, replace the cover and complete the cooking.

The piquant taste of red cabbage will improve if, after it has cooled, it is allowed to rest for a day in the refrigerator and then reheated either on top of the stove or in a 325° oven. In any case, serve hot, as an accompaniment to a stuffed loin of pork or goose *(page 24)* to complete the traditional Danish Christmas dinner.

Rårakor med Gräslök

LACY POTATO PANCAKES WITH CHIVES (SWEDISH)

To serve 4

4 medium-sized baking potatoes
2 tablespoons chopped fresh chives

2 teaspoons salt
Freshly ground black pepper
2 to 4 tablespoons butter
2 to 4 tablespoons vegetable oil

Peel the potatoes and grate them coarsely, preferably into tiny slivers, into a large mixing bowl. Do not drain off the potato water that will accumulate in the bowl. Working quickly to prevent the potatoes from turning brown, mix into them the chopped chives, salt and a few grindings of pepper.

Heat the butter and oil in a 10- to 12-inch skillet over high heat until the foam subsides. The pan must be very hot, but not smoking. Using 2 tablespoons of potato mixture for each pancake, fry 3 or 4 at a time, flattening them with a spatula to about 3 inches in diameter. Fry each batch over medium-high heat for 2 or 3 minutes on each side, or until they are crisp and golden. Add more butter and oil, if necessary, after each batch.

Pinaattiohukaiset

SPINACH PANCAKES (FINNISH)

To serve 6 to 8

1½ cups milk
1 teaspoon salt
⅛ teaspoon nutmeg
1 cup flour
2 tablespoons unsalted butter, melted
2 eggs

½ teaspoon sugar
½ pound freshly cooked spinach,
    squeezed dry and finely chopped,
    or substitute 1 nine-ounce package
    frozen chopped spinach, thoroughly
    defrosted, squeezed dry, and again
    chopped
1 to 2 tablespoons butter, softened

In a large mixing bowl, combine the milk, salt, nutmeg and flour and then stir in the melted butter. (Or, if you prefer to use an electric blender, all of these ingredients can be mixed at once at medium speed.) In a separate bowl, combine the eggs and sugar and stir this into the batter. Gradually add the chopped spinach.

With a pastry brush or paper towel, coat the bottom of a heavy 10- to 12-inch skillet with about a teaspoon of soft butter and set the skillet over moderately high heat. When the pan is very hot, drop 2 tablespoons of the batter onto the skillet and with a spoon or spatula, spread it out evenly to form a 3-inch disk. Cook the pancakes—3 or 4 at a time—for 2 to 3 minutes on each side, or until they have browned lightly. Keep them warm on a heated platter covered loosely with aluminum foil. Add more butter to the skillet as it becomes necessary while cooking the remaining pancakes. Serve the spinach pancakes as a vegetable course—accompanied, if you like, by lingonberries.

Bruna Bönor

SWEETENED BROWN BEANS (SWEDISH)

To serve 4

1¾ cups imported Swedish
   dried brown beans
5 cups water

1½ teaspoons salt
½ cup white vinegar
½ cup dark corn syrup
1 tablespoon dark brown sugar

Wash the beans thoroughly in cold running water. Since the beans will expand considerably as they soak, put them in a large pot with 5 cups of cold water. Bring to a boil, turn off the heat and let the beans soak, uncovered, for at least 1 hour (or you may soak them overnight in cold water and omit the boiling process). Whichever method you choose to cook the beans, bring the soaked beans to a boil in their soaking water, then half cover the pot and simmer over very low heat for 1 hour. Stir in the salt, vinegar, corn syrup and brown sugar, and continue cooking slowly. The beans should be tender in another hour, and the sauce should be brown and thick. However, dried beans vary enormously in their moisture content, and the cooking time may be longer or shorter by as much as half an hour. To make certain that the beans do not overcook, test by eating one occasionally.

If the cooking liquid evaporates too much before the beans are done, add a little water. If, on the other hand, the sauce has not thickened sufficiently by the time the beans are almost done, boil them rapidly, uncovered, over high heat to reduce the liquid.

This dish is often served with slices of Canadian (back) bacon or boiled sausage.

Paistetut Sienet

FRIED MUSHROOMS IN SOUR CREAM (FINNISH)

To serve 4

4 tablespoons butter
¼ cup finely chopped onions

1 pound fresh mushrooms, thinly
  sliced
¼ cup dry bread crumbs
½ cup sour cream

In a heavy 10- to 12-inch stainless-steel or enameled skillet, melt 4 table-spoons of butter over moderate heat. When the foam subsides, add the chopped onions and cook 3 to 5 minutes, or until the onions are soft and transparent but not brown. Now add the mushroom slices and cook another 3 to 5 minutes. Shake the pan from time to time so that the mushrooms do not stick. When the mushrooms are a light, delicate brown, sprinkle in the bread crumbs and toss the contents of the pan gently with a rubber spatula or wooden spoon. Remove the pan from the heat.

In a small bowl, beat the sour cream with a wooden spoon or whisk for a minute or two, then stir it into the skillet. Toss lightly until the mush-rooms are well coated with the cream. Serve as a vegetable accompaniment to meat or fish dishes.

Grønlangkaal

KALE IN CREAM SAUCE (DANISH)

To serve 6 to 8

1 pound kale
2 teaspoons salt
4 tablespoons butter

4 tablespoons flour
1 cup milk
1 cup heavy cream
½ teaspoon freshly ground black
  pepper

Discard the tough outer stalks of the kale and wash the leaves carefully under cold running water, shaking to remove any sand. Shake the kale again to remove excess water, and tear it into large pieces. Place the kale in a 4- to 6-quart saucepan with ½ teaspoon of the salt and just enough cold water to barely cover it. Cook, tightly covered, over medium heat for about 15 minutes, or until the kale is very tender (test by tasting a leaf). Drain the kale through a sieve, pressing down on the vegetable with a large spoon to extract all of the moisture. Then chop very fine.

In a heavy 2- to 3-quart saucepan, prepare the following sauce. Melt the butter over medium heat; remove the pan from the heat and stir in the flour. Now add the milk and cream all at once, beating vigorously with a wire whisk. Return the pan to low heat and cook, whisking constantly, until the sauce comes to a boil and is smooth and thick. Add the remaining salt, pepper and the chopped kale, taste for seasoning if necessary and cook for another 1 or 2 minutes, or until the kale is heated through.

This hearty vegetable is traditionally served as a part of a substantial winter dinner with a main dish such as roast pork and caramel potatoes (*pages 34 and 49*).

Länttulaatikko
RUTABAGA CASSEROLE (FINNISH)

To serve 8

2½ pounds (about 2) rutabagas, peeled and cut into ¼-inch dice (8 cups), or substitute 2½ pounds white or yellow turnips, peeled and diced
3 teaspoons salt
¼ cup dry bread crumbs

¼ cup heavy cream
½ teaspoon nutmeg
2 eggs, lightly beaten
2 teaspoons soft butter
2 tablespoons plus 2 teaspoons soft butter
2 tablespoons butter, cut into tiny bits

Preheat the oven to 350°. Place the 8 cups of diced rutabagas (or diced turnips) in a 4- to 6-quart stainless-steel or enameled saucepan. Pour in enough cold water to just cover the vegetables, add 1 teaspoon of salt and bring to a boil. Lower the heat and simmer, partially covered, for 15 to 20 minutes, or until the rutabagas offer no resistance when pierced with the tip of a sharp knife.

Drain the rutabagas and, with the back of a spoon, force them through a sieve set over a bowl. In another bowl, soak the bread crumbs in the heavy cream for a few minutes. Stir in the nutmeg, 2 teaspoons of the salt and lightly beaten eggs, then add the puréed rutabagas and mix together thoroughly. Stir in 2 tablespoons of the soft butter.

Spread a 2- to 2½-quart casserole or baking dish with the remaining 2 teaspoons of soft butter and transfer the rutabaga mixture to the casserole. Dot with the bits of butter and bake uncovered for 1 hour, or until the top is lightly browned.

Desserts

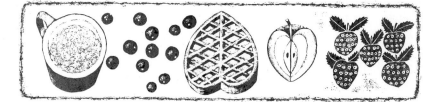

Mansikkalumi
STRAWBERRY SNOW (FINNISH)

To serve 6 to 8

2 cups fresh, hulled strawberries or
   substitute 2 ten-ounce packages
   frozen whole strawberries,
   thoroughly defrosted and drained

½ cup sugar
4 egg whites
Pinch of salt
¾ cup heavy cream, stiffly whipped
12 to 16 whole strawberries, fresh or
   frozen

With the back of a large spoon, rub the fresh or thoroughly defrosted frozen strawberries through a fine sieve into a small mixing bowl. Stir into this purée the ½ cup of sugar, a little at a time.

Using a balloon-type wire whisk, beat the egg whites and salt vigorously in a large bowl (preferably of unlined copper) until the whites are stiff enough to form unwavering peaks when the beater is lifted out of the bowl. With a gentle under-over cutting motion rather than a stirring motion, use a rubber spatula to fold first the strawberry purée and then the whipped cream into the egg whites. Pour the strawberry snow into an attractive serving bowl, or individual dessert bowls, and decorate with the whole strawberries. This dessert can be served at once, or it may be refrigerated for a few hours and served later in the day.

Omenalumi
APPLE SNOW (FINNISH)

To serve 6 to 8

4 egg whites
Pinch of salt
½ cup sugar

2 cups tart applesauce, freshly made,
   canned or bottled
½ teaspoon lemon juice
⅛ teaspoon cinnamon

With a large, balloon whisk, beat the egg whites and the pinch of salt in a large mixing bowl (preferably of unlined copper) until they begin to foam. Gradually add the sugar and continue to beat vigorously until the whites are stiff enough to form unwavering peaks when the beater is lifted out of the bowl. (A rotary or electric beater may be easier to use, but the whites will not rise so voluminously nor have so fine a texture.)

In a separate bowl, combine the applesauce and lemon juice. Stir a heaping tablespoon of the beaten egg whites into the applesauce to lighten it. Then, with a rubber spatula, gently fold in the rest of the whites, using an under-over cutting motion rather than a rotary motion. Turn the apple snow into a serving bowl and sprinkle the top with cinnamon.

NOTE: The Finns serve apple snow as soon as it is made, but it can be frozen effectively in ice-cube trays and served as an ice.

Tippaleivät
MAY DAY CRULLERS (FINNISH)

To make 14 to 16 crullers

2 tablespoons lukewarm water
½ package (1½ teaspoons) active
    dry yeast
1 cup lukewarm milk (110° to 115°)

2 eggs
1½ teaspoons sugar
½ teaspoon salt
2 cups flour
Vegetable oil for deep-fat frying
Confectioners' sugar

Put the 2 tablespoons of lukewarm water into a small bowl and sprinkle in the yeast. Let it stand 2 or 3 minutes, then stir until the yeast is dissolved. Set the bowl in a warm, draft-free place (such as an unlighted oven) for 3 to 5 minutes, or until the yeast bubbles and the mixture doubles. Now stir in the lukewarm milk. In a large bowl, stir the eggs and sugar only long enough to combine them. Pour in the yeast mixture and, stirring briskly with a spoon, add the salt. Beat in the flour, ½ cup at a time, beating vigorously until a soft batter is formed. Cover with a kitchen towel and set in a warm place (again, the unlighted oven) for 1 hour, or until the batter has doubled in bulk, but do not let it stand longer.

Pour enough oil into a deep-fat fryer or heavy 10- to 12-inch skillet to reach a depth of about 2 inches, and place over medium-high heat until the oil is very hot and a light haze forms above it. Spoon 1 cup of the batter into a pastry bag fitted with a ¼-inch plain tip. Holding the bag upright, squeeze the batter into the hot fat in a 3- to 4-inch circle, moving the bag in a circle to build a "bird's nest" of 2 or 3 rings more or less atop one another. Deep-fry 2 or 3 crullers at a time, turning them over with a spatula or tongs after 1 minute, or when they are a golden brown. Fry the other side, then remove from the fat with a slotted spoon and drain on paper towels. When the crullers are cool, sift the confectioners' sugar over them and serve with coffee or *sima (page 86)*.

Himmelsk Lapskaus

FRUIT POTPOURRI WITH BRANDY OR RUM EGG SAUCE (NORWEGIAN)

To serve 4 to 6

FRUIT POTPOURRI

¾ cup chopped bananas	½ cup chopped walnuts or pecans
¾ cup halved seedless grapes	1 cup chopped apples or oranges

Toss the fruits and nuts together in a serving bowl and chill before serving with *eggedosis*, the rich egg sauce described below. In Norway this sauce is frequently served alone. Although American palates may find it excessively sweet by itself, it is an excellent foil for the tartness of fresh fruits.

EGGEDOSIS

5 egg yolks	5 tablespoons sugar
2 egg whites	1 tablespoon brandy or rum

EGGEDOSIS: With an electric mixer set at high speed, whip together the 5 egg yolks, 2 egg whites and sugar. When the mixture has thickened to a custardlike consistency, add the brandy (or rum). To make by hand, whip the yolks and whites to a froth with a wire whisk before gradually beating in the sugar. Continue to beat vigorously until the mixture thickens; then beat in the liquor. Serve immediately in a chilled dish along with the fruit.

Rødgrød med Fløde

RED FRUIT PUDDING WITH CREAM (DANISH)

To serve 6

	2 tablespoons sugar
1½ pounds of fresh raspberries or	2 tablespoons arrowroot powder
strawberries, or a combination	¼ cup cold water
of the two (or substitute 2-ten-	Slivered almonds
ounce packages of frozen berries)	½ cup light cream

Remove any hulls from the fresh berries, wash the berries quickly in a sieve, drain and spread them out on paper towels, and pat them dry. Cut the larger berries into quarters and place them in the container of an electric blender. Whirl at high speed for 2 or 3 minutes until they are puréed. If you are using frozen berries, defrost them thoroughly, then purée them in the blender—juices and all. To make the dessert by hand, rub the contents of the packages, or the fresh berries, through a fine sieve set over a large mixing bowl. Place the berry purée (which should measure about 2⅓ cups) in a 1- to 1½-quart enameled or stainless-steel saucepan and stir in the sugar. Bring to a boil, stirring constantly. Mix the 2 tablespoons of arrowroot and the cold water to a smooth paste, and stir it into the pan. Let the mixture come to a simmer to thicken the jelly (do not let it boil), then remove the pan from the heat.

Pour into individual dessert bowls or a large serving bowl. Chill for at least 2 hours. Before serving the *rødgrød*, decorate the top with a few slivers of almonds and pass a pitcher of light cream separately.

Rabarbragrøt
RHUBARB COMPOTE (NORWEGIAN)

To serve 6 or 8

2 cups water
¾ cup sugar
1½ pounds rhubarb, washed, scraped
    and cut into ½-inch pieces (about
    4 cups)
½ teaspoon vanilla

3 tablespoons cornstarch
¼ cup cold water

WHIPPED CREAM (optional)
1 cup chilled heavy cream
¼ cup sugar
1 teaspoon vanilla

Dissolve the sugar in the water in a 2-quart enameled or stainless-steel saucepan, and bring to a boil. Drop in the rhubarb, reduce the heat to low and simmer, uncovered, for 20 to 30 minutes, or until the rhubarb shows no resistance when pierced with the tip of a sharp knife. Remove the pan from the heat and stir in the vanilla.

In a small bowl, mix the cornstarch with the cold water to a smooth paste. Gradually stir it into the stewed rhubarb, and bring it to a boil, stirring constantly. Simmer about 3 to 5 minutes, or until the mixture has thickened. Pour into a serving bowl and chill.

Although *rabarbragrøt* has a sweet flavor, with a slightly tart edge, many Norwegians prefer it even sweeter—and often garnish it with whipped cream. Make the whipped cream no more than 1 hour before you plan to serve the dessert. Beat the chilled heavy cream in a large chilled bowl with a wire whisk or a hand or electric beater until it begins to thicken. Add the sugar and vanilla and continue to beat until it is just about firm enough to hold its shape. Mask the rhubarb in the bowl with the whipped cream, or squeeze the cream through a pastry tube in decorative swirls.

Fløtevafler

SOUR-CREAM WAFFLES (NORWEGIAN)

Makes 6 waffles

5 eggs
½ cup sugar
1 cup flour, sifted

1 teaspoon ground cardamom
  or ginger
1 cup sour cream
4 tablespoons unsalted butter, melted

Beat the eggs and sugar together for 5 to 10 minutes in an electric mixer or by hand with a wire whisk until it falls back into the bowl in a lazy ribbon when the beater is lifted out. Now, with a rubber spatula, alternately fold in half the flour, cardamom (or ginger), and sour cream, and then the remaining flour. Lightly stir in the melted butter and set the batter aside for 10 minutes. If you use a nonelectric Norwegian waffle iron, heat it, ungreased, until it is so hot that a drop of water sputters when flicked across its surface. Pour about ¾ cup of the batter in the center of the hot iron, close the top and cook over direct heat for 5 minutes on each side. Serve with lingonberry or another tart jam. This batter may be used in any regular American electric waffle iron and cooked according to the instructions for that iron.

Ris à l'Amande

RICE AND ALMOND DESSERT (DANISH)

To serve 6 to 8

1 quart milk
3½ tablespoons sugar
¾ cup long-grain white rice

¾ cup blanched and chopped almonds
¼ cup sherry
2 teaspoons vanilla
½ pint chilled heavy cream

Bring the milk to a boil in a 2-quart saucepan and add the sugar and rice. Stir once or twice, then lower the heat and simmer uncovered about 25 minutes, or until the rice is quite soft but not mushy. (Cooking time for rice varies, but a sure test is to rub a grain between the thumb and forefinger; if there is no hard kernel in the center, the rice is done.) Pour the finished rice immediately into a shallow bowl to cool it quickly, and then add the chopped almonds, sherry and vanilla.

Whip the heavy cream in a chilled bowl with a wire whisk or hand or electric beater until it thickens and holds its shape softly. Fold it into the tepid rice mixture, turn the pudding into a serving dish and chill before serving.

A cold cherry or raspberry sauce or a spoonful of cherry liqueur is often served on top of this modern version of an ancient Christmas porridge.

Plättar

SWEDISH PANCAKES

This is a famous Scandinavian dish, customarily served with lingonberries or fruit preserves. In Sweden, it is part of the traditional Thursday night dinner, following the main dish of pea soup with pork (page 9).

To serve 6 to 8

3 eggs

2 cups milk or 1 cup of milk and 1 cup of light cream

1 cup flour

6 tablespoons unsalted butter, melted

½ teaspoon salt

Beat the eggs together with ½ cup of milk for 2 or 3 minutes with a rotary beater or whisk. Add the flour all at once and beat to a heavy, smooth consistency. Beat in the remaining milk and then the melted butter and salt. Because of the large amount of butter in the batter, the skillet will require little, if any, additional buttering.

If you have the Swedish 5- or 7-section pancake pan, heat it, ungreased, over medium-high heat. When the pan is so hot that a few drops of water flicked on its surface bounce around and evaporate instantly, drop a tablespoon of batter into each depression. The pancakes should bubble almost immediately. After 1 or 2 minutes, when the edges begin to brown, turn the pancakes with a narrow spatula and cook another 1 or 2 minutes to brown the other side.

A heavy cast-iron skillet can be used as successfully as the sectioned pan, but first grease it lightly with a pastry brush or paper towel dipped into a little melted butter (this step need not be repeated). When the skillet is very hot, drop 1 tablespoon of batter into the pan for each pancake; each should form a 3-inch circle. When the edges brown lightly after about 1 minute, turn the pancakes with a spatula and cook another minute or two. In Swedish families, the *plättar* are served "from pan to plate," but if necessary, set each batch of pancakes aside on a platter and keep them warm in a 200° oven while you complete the rest.

Äppelkaka
APPLE CAKE (SWEDISH)

To serve 4 to 6

8 tablespoons (1 quarter-pound stick)
  unsalted butter
3 cups dry bread crumbs
3 tablespoons sugar

1½ teaspoons cinnamon
2 teaspoons soft butter
2½ cups applesauce,
  canned or freshly made
2 tablespoons unsalted butter,
  cut into ¼-inch bits

In a heavy 8- to 10-inch skillet, melt the 8 tablespoons of butter over moderate heat. When the foam subsides, add the bread crumbs and the sugar and cinnamon, and stir with a wooden spoon. Continue stirring for 3 to 5 minutes, or until the mixture is evenly but lightly browned.

Preheat the oven to 375°. With a pastry brush or paper towel, spread a 1-quart mold, soufflé dish or deep cake pan with the 2 teaspoons of soft butter and cover the bottom with a ½-inch layer of the browned crumbs. Pour on a thick layer of the applesauce, then another of bread crumbs, alternating until all of the bread crumbs and applesauce are used. Top with a layer of bread crumbs, and dot with the 2 tablespoons of butter cut into small bits. Bake for 25 minutes in the center of the oven, then remove from the oven and let the cake cool to room temperature. Serve alone or with cold vanilla sauce *(page 46)*.

Vatkattu Marjapuuro
WHIPPED BERRY PUDDING (FINNISH)

To serve 6 to 8

3 cups bottled or canned cranberry
  juice

6 tablespoons sugar
½ cup uncooked Cream-of-Wheat

In a 1½- to 2-quart saucepan, bring the cranberry juice to a boil over moderate heat. While the juice boils, sprinkle in the sugar, a little at a time, and then slowly add the Cream-of-Wheat, stirring briskly with a wooden spoon. Reduce the heat and simmer for 6 to 8 minutes, stirring occasionally, until the mixture becomes a thick purée.

With a rubber spatula, transfer the purée from the saucepan to a large mixing bowl. Use an electric mixer for the next step. (Although it is possible to make *vatkattu marjapuuro* with a wire whisk, it is scarcely practical; an hour of vigorous whisking might be required.) Beat with the mixer set at high speed for 10 to 15 minutes, or until the pudding has doubled in volume, is a delicate pink color and is light and fluffy. Pour into a large serving bowl, or individual dessert bowls, and serve as soon as possible.

NOTE: If you wish to make this dessert with a nontart juice such as apple, strawberry or raspberry, add a tablespoon of lemon juice.

Bondepige med Slør
VEILED COUNTRY LASS (DANISH)

To serve 4 to 6

8 tablespoons (1 quarter-pound stick) unsalted butter
3 cups fine, dry bread crumbs made from dark rye or pumpernickel bread
3 tablespoons sugar
2 tablespoons grated semisweet

baking chocolate
1 tablespoon butter, softened
2½ cups applesauce, canned or homemade
2 tablespoons unsalted butter, cut into ¼-inch bits
1 cup chilled heavy cream
2 to 3 tablespoons raspberry jam (optional)

In a heavy 10- to 12-inch skillet, melt the 8 tablespoons of butter over moderate heat. When the foam subsides, add the bread crumbs and sugar and stir with a wooden spoon. Turn down the heat to low and continue stirring until the mixture is evenly browned and the bread crumbs are dry and crisp. Remove from the heat, stir in the grated chocolate and mix until thoroughly melted. Set the pan aside to cool a little.

Preheat the oven to 375°. Lightly grease a shallow 1-quart mold, soufflé dish or cake pan with the 1 tablespoon of soft butter, and cover the bottom of the dish with a ½-inch layer of the browned crumbs. Spoon on a thick layer of the applesauce, then another of bread crumbs, alternating until all of the ingredients have been used. Top with a layer of crumbs and dot with the 2 tablespoons of butter cut into ¼-inch bits. Bake for 25 minutes in the center of the oven and let the cake cool to room temperature.

Shortly before serving, beat the chilled heavy cream in a large chilled mixing bowl with a wire whisk, hand or electric beater until it just holds its shape. Use the whipped cream to top the cake, and decorate, if you wish, with dabs of the raspberry jam.

Hovdessert
MERINGUES WITH CHOCOLATE SAUCE (SWEDISH)

Makes 18 to 20

MERINGUES	1 cup superfine sugar
4 egg whites (at room temperature)	1 tablespoon soft butter
Pinch of salt	2 tablespoons flour

MERINGUES: Preheat the oven to 250°. In a large bowl, beat the egg whites and salt with a wire balloon whisk or a rotary or electric beater until the mixture is foamy. Gradually beat in the sugar and continue beating for at least 5 minutes, or until the egg whites are very stiff and form solid, unwavering peaks when the whisk is lifted out of the bowl.

With a pastry brush or paper towels, grease a cookie sheet with the soft butter, sprinkle it with flour and shake the pan to coat it evenly. Now turn the pan over and tap it against a hard surface to knock off any excess flour.

Drop mounds of meringue (about 1 tablespoon) onto the cookie sheet. The mounds should be about 2 inches high and 1 inch wide; their shape and size will not alter in the baking process. Set the cookie sheet in the middle of the oven for 50 minutes. This is actually a drying rather than a true baking process and the meringues should remain as colorless as possible. If they seem to be taking on color, turn the oven down to 200°. They should be dry and crisp, but tender, when they are done. Serve with the following sauce.

CHOCOLATE SAUCE	¾ cup water
1 cup sugar	1 cup unsweetened cocoa

CHOCOLATE SAUCE: Bring the sugar and water to a rolling boil in a heavy saucepan and boil briskly for 2 minutes. Remove the pan from the heat and add all of the cocoa, beating rapidly with a wire whisk until the sauce is smooth and satiny. Spoon about 1 tablespoon over each meringue. (Two meringues per person is a customary serving.) This sauce may also be served hot or cold over ice cream, or used as a cold syrup to make chocolate milk or hot cocoa.

Fransk Äppelkaka
BAKED APPLE HALVES WITH ALMOND TOPPING (SWEDISH)

To serve 6

2 cups cold water
¼ lemon
4 large tart cooking apples
½ cup sugar
2 teaspoons unsalted butter, softened

¼ pound unsalted butter, softened
⅔ cup sugar
3 egg yolks
½ cup ground blanched almonds
2 teaspoons lemon juice
3 egg whites
Pinch of salt

In a 1½- to 2-quart saucepan, combine the cold water, the juice of the lemon quarter and the lemon quarter itself. Halve, peel and core each apple and, as you proceed, drop the halves into the lemon-water to prevent discoloration. Then stir the sugar into the water. Bring it quickly to the boil, stirring occasionally, lower the heat and simmer uncovered for 6 to 8 minutes, or until the apples are tender. Remove them from the pan and drain on a cake rack.

Preheat the oven to 350°. With a pastry brush or paper towel, grease a shallow baking dish (just large enough to hold the apples in one layer) with the 2 teaspoons of soft butter. Place the apple halves in it side by side, cut side down. Cream the ¼ pound of butter by using an electric beater set at medium speed, or by beating it against the sides of a bowl with a wooden spoon until it is smooth. Now beat in the ⅔ cup of sugar, a little at a time, then the egg yolks one by one, and last the almonds and lemon juice. With a balloon whisk or electric beater, beat the egg whites with a pinch of salt in a large mixing bowl (preferably of unlined copper) until they form stiff, unwavering peaks. Mix 2 tablespoons of the stiff egg whites into the creamed sugar-butter-egg mixture, then gently fold the remaining mixture into the egg whites with a rubber spatula, using an under-over rather than a stirring motion. Spread the almond topping lightly over the poached apples and bake in the center of the oven for about 20 minutes, or until the surface is golden. Serve at room temperature.

Bread, Cakes and Cookies

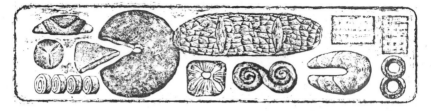

Fyllda Strutar
PASTRY CONES FILLED WITH WHIPPED CREAM AND BERRIES (SWEDISH)

To make 16 to 18

2 eggs
⅓ cup superfine sugar
3 tablespoons flour
2 teaspoons soft butter

1 tablespoon flour
1 cup chilled heavy cream
1 tablespoon sugar
1 teaspoon vanilla
16 to 18 fresh strawberries or ¾ cup
    lingonberries

Preheat the oven to 400°. In a large mixing bowl, beat together the eggs and sugar until they are thoroughly combined. Now stir in the flour, a little at a time, and mix until smooth. Lightly grease a cookie sheet with the 2 teaspoons of soft butter and sprinkle it with flour, tipping the sheet to coat it evenly. Turn the sheet over and tap it lightly against a table or counter to knock off any excess flour.

Place 2 tablespoons of the batter on the cookie sheet and with the back of a large spoon or a rubber spatula, spread the batter out to form a thin circle about 4½ inches in diameter. (Do not place more than 3 or 4 circles on the sheet; they dry out rapidly after having been baked and must be relatively moist if they are to be successfully formed into cones.) Set the cookie sheet in the middle of the oven and bake 6 to 8 minutes, or until the circles are a pale gold around the edges. Now quickly lift a circle loose from the cookie sheet with the flat of a metal spatula. Holding the circle gently in both hands, fold the two sides toward the center to form a cone. Stand the cone up in a water glass and let it remain there for 1 or 2 minutes, until it has dried and holds its shape. Now quickly shape the remaining baked circles, replacing the cookie sheet in the oven for a minute if the pastry has cooled too much and become brittle. Repeat with the remaining batter, using a newly greased and floured cookie sheet for each batch you prepare.

The *strutar* can be baked several days in advance and kept crisp in airtight containers. Just before you are ready to serve the cones—as a dessert or confection—whip the chilled heavy cream with a wire whisk, rotary or electric beater in a large chilled bowl until it begins to thicken. Add the sugar and vanilla and continue to beat until it is firm enough to hold its shape. Spoon the whipped cream into the cones (or pipe it in with a pastry bag) and top each with a strawberry or a few lingonberries. A traditional and practical way of serving the cones is to place a drinking glass in the center of a shallow round bowl. Place 1 cone in the glass, then circle it with the others, leaning them against the glass.

NOTE: Forming the cone does take practice and some dexterity. For a simpler, but equally delicate dessert—a pastry sandwich—prepare the batter as above. Then place 1 tablespoon of batter on the buttered and floured cookie sheets and spread it into a 2-inch circle. Bake a dozen or so circles at a time, for 4 to 5 minutes, lift them from the cookie sheet with a metal spatula, and let them cool on a wire cake rack. When ready to serve, spread the whipped cream over half of the circles and cover them with the remaining circles.

Havregrynskage
OAT CAKES (DANISH)

To make 12

	¼ cup sugar
8 tablespoons (1 quarter-pound stick)	2 cups instant oatmeal
unsalted butter	¼ cup white corn syrup

Melt the butter in a heavy 10- to 12-inch skillet over moderate heat and stir in the sugar with a wooden spoon. Let them bubble together for 20 seconds, taking care not to let the butter burn. Add the oatmeal and, stirring occasionally, cook for 5 to 10 minutes, or until the oatmeal is golden brown. Remove from heat and stir in the white corn syrup.

Rinse custard cups or the small cups (approximately 2½ inches in diameter) of a muffin tin with cold water and shake out the excess moisture. Pack the bottom and sides of the cups or muffin pans firmly with the oatmeal mixture, dividing it equally. Refrigerate for at least three hours. Loosen the cakes from their containers by running a knife around the edges; gently slide them out and serve with cold buttermilk soup *(page 8)*. (In Denmark the cakes are sometimes split and served with the soup poured over them.)

Äppelformar
APPLE MUFFINS (SWEDISH)

Makes 12 muffins

5 tablespoons unsalted butter
½ cup sugar
1 egg
1½ cups all-purpose flour
¼ teaspoon baking powder

FILLING
1½ cups applesauce

ALTERNATE FRUIT FILLING
2 tablespoons unsalted butter
2 tart cooking apples, peeled, cored
   and diced finely (about 2 cups)
¾ cup apricot preserves
Slivered almonds
Confectioners' sugar

Cream the butter and sugar together by using an electric mixer set at medium speed or by beating them against the sides of a bowl with a wooden spoon until light and fluffy. Beat in the egg. Sift the flour and baking powder together and add to the butter mixture, using your fingertips to blend all the ingredients into a dough. Shape into a ball, wrap in wax paper and chill for at least 1 hour.

Preheat the oven to 350°. The *äppelformar* are made in muffin tins of 12 cups, each of which is 2 or 2½ inches in diameter. Lightly oil or butter the cups. Cut off ⅓ of the dough, rewrap it and replace it in the refrigerator. Divide the remaining dough into 12 pieces and firmly press each piece into the bottom and sides of the cups with your fingers. The dough lining should be about ¼ inch thick. Fill each cup with 2 tablespoons of applesauce. Roll out the remaining chilled dough to a ⅛-inch thickness and, using a 2- or 2½-inch cookie cutter or glass, cut the dough into 12 circles the same diameter as the muffin cups. Moisten the edges of the muffin tops with cold water and pinch them together with the edges of the filled muffins, sealing them completely. Bake for 30 to 35 minutes. Loosen the muffins gently with a knife and let them cool in the cups. Use a narrow spatula or knife to lift them out. Sprinkle with confectioners' sugar before serving.

ALTERNATE FRUIT FILLING: Melt the butter in an enameled or stainless-steel saucepan over moderate heat and add the finely diced apples. Cook 1 or 2 minutes, shaking the pan to coat the apples in the butter. Line the muffin cups with dough, as above, and fill each almost full with the apples. Top each with 1 tablespoon of apricot preserves and a sprinkling of slivered almonds. Cover with the muffin tops and bake as above.

Spritsar

SPRITZ RING COOKIES (SWEDISH)

To make 6 dozen cookies

2 egg yolks

16 tablespoons (2 quarter-pound
    sticks) unsalted butter, softened
¾ cup sugar

1 teaspoon almond extract
2½ cups all-purpose flour
¼ teaspoon salt

In a large mixing bowl, cream the butter and sugar together with an electric mixer set at medium speed or by beating them with a wooden spoon until light and fluffy. Then add the egg yolks and almond extract. Sift the flour and salt together and add it a third at a time to the creamed mixture, beating it well after each addition with a wooden spoon.

Preheat the oven to 400°. Place the dough in a pastry bag fitted with a small star tip. Force the dough out onto an ungreased cookie sheet in S or O shapes about 2 inches in diameter. Bake for 10 or 12 minutes, or until the cookies are a light gold. Immediately remove them to a cake rack with a wide spatula. The cooked *spritsar* can be stored for several weeks in tightly sealed tins.

Mor Monsen's Kaker

MOTHER MONSEN'S CAKES (NORWEGIAN)

To make about 2 dozen small cakes

4 eggs
2 cups flour

2 teaspoons unsalted butter, softened
1 pound unsalted butter, softened
2 cups sugar

1 teaspoon vanilla
½ cup finely chopped blanched almonds
¼ cup dried currants

Preheat the oven to 375°. With a pastry brush or paper towel, spread a 12-by-18-inch jelly-roll pan with 2 teaspoons of butter. Cream the butter and sugar together by beating them against the side of a bowl with a wooden spoon or by using an electric mixer set at medium speed. When light and fluffy, beat in the eggs, 1 at a time. Then beat in the flour and vanilla. Spread the batter evenly onto the pan, sprinkle the surface with the almonds and currants and bake 20 to 25 minutes, until the surface is a light gold. Remove from the oven and let the cake cool in the pan. With a sharp knife, cut into small triangles or squares.

These cakes, frequently served at Norwegian Christmases, can be made 2 weeks before the feast, but they must then be wrapped in aluminum foil or placed in an airtight tin and stored in a cool place.

Jødekager I
JEWISH CAKES (DANISH)

To make about 3 dozen cookies

2½ cups flour
½ teaspoon salt
16 tablespoons (2 quarter-pound sticks)
  unsalted butter
¾ cup sugar
1 egg

1 teaspoon baking powder
1 egg white, lightly beaten
¼ cup cinnamon and ¼ cup granulated
  sugar combined

Cream the butter and sugar together by using an electric mixer set at medium speed or by beating them with a wooden spoon until light and fluffy. Beat in the egg. Sift together the flour, salt and baking powder and beat into the creamed butter, ½ cup at a time. Continue to beat until thoroughly mixed. Then form into a ball, wrap in wax paper and chill for several hours.

Preheat the oven to 400°. Divide the chilled dough in thirds. On a lightly floured pastry board, roll out each third of dough into a circle about ⅛ inch thick. Using a 2- or 3-inch cookie cutter, cut the dough into rounds. Gather up the excess dough, roll it out again, and cut out additional rounds. Lay the rounds side by side on a lightly greased cookie sheet, and, with a pastry brush, spread the tops lightly with the beaten egg white. Then sprinkle with the cinnamon-sugar mixture. Bake 2 sheets of cookies at a time in the center of the oven for about 8 minutes. Remove from the oven and, with a spatula, immediately transfer the cookies to a cake rack. Let them cool thoroughly before storing them in airtight tins.

Jødekager II
JEWISH CAKES (DANISH)

To make about 3 dozen cookies

1 teaspoon grated lemon peel
12 tablespoons chilled unsalted butter,
  cut in ¼-inch bits
1 cup sifted flour
1 cup dark brown sugar
⅛ teaspoon baking powder
Pinch of ground cardamom

1 egg yolk, lightly beaten
Flour
1 egg white, lightly beaten
½ cup combined equal parts of
  cinnamon, sugar and finely chopped
  almonds

In a large chilled mixing bowl, combine the butter and flour. Working quickly, use your fingertips to rub the flour and butter together until they have the appearance of flakes of coarse meal. Work in the sugar, baking powder and cardamom, add the grated lemon peel and egg yolk, and mix together thoroughly until the ingredients can be gathered together into a compact ball. Wrap it in wax paper and refrigerate for at least 3 hours, or until it is firm.

Preheat the oven to 400°. Remove the dough from the refrigerator 5 or 10 minutes before rolling it out. If it seems hard, tap it all over with a rolling pin. Roll the dough into a sheet ⅛ inch thick on a floured pastry board and cut it into large rounds with a 3- or 4-inch cookie cutter or wine glass. Place the cookies about ½ inch apart on lightly greased cookie sheets and brush them with the beaten egg white. Sprinkle with the combined cinnamon sugar and almonds and bake the cookies in the middle of the oven for 8 minutes, or until they are a light brown. Remove them at once from the baking sheets with a spatula and cool the cookies on a wire cake rack before storing them in airtight containers.

Brune Kager
LITTLE BROWN CAKES (DANISH)

To make about 6 dozen cookies

1½ cups flour

½ cup dark corn syrup
5 tablespoons dark brown sugar
4 tablespoons unsalted butter
½ teaspoon baking soda

1 teaspoon powdered cloves
1¼ teaspoons ground cardamom
1¼ teaspoons grated lemon peel
3 ounces whole blanched almonds

Heat the corn syrup, brown sugar and butter in a heavy saucepan until the sugar is thoroughly dissolved. Do not let it boil. Remove from the heat and let it cool. Meanwhile, sift the baking soda, flour and powdered cloves together into a large bowl. Add the cardamom, grated lemon peel and the lukewarm syrup and knead the dough well by pressing it down with the heel of your hand, turning it, folding it over and pressing again. Continue kneading for 5 to 10 minutes, until the dough is smooth and shiny. Wrap in wax paper and set aside in a cool place for at least 2 hours.

Preheat the oven to 400°. On a lightly floured surface, roll the dough into a sheet ⅛ inch thick, then with a cookie cutter or small wine glass cut it into 2-inch rounds. Grease a cookie sheet and lay the cookies on it about an inch apart. Lightly press 1 almond into the center of each and bake 5 to 6 minutes, or until they are a light gold. Cool the brune kager on the cookie sheet. The cookies can be stored for several weeks in tightly sealed tins.

Wienerbrød

Makes 2 cakes or about 2 dozen pastries

½ cup lukewarm water	1 tablespoon unsalted butter
2 packages active dry yeast	2 whole eggs
½ cup sugar	1 teaspoon salt
5 to 6 cups unsifted all-purpose flour	¼ teaspoon ground cardamom
or 6 to 7 cups granulated flour	1 teaspoon vanilla
½ cup cold milk	1 pound unsalted butter, chilled

Pour the lukewarm water into a small bowl and sprinkle the yeast and 1 teaspoon of the sugar over it. Let the mixture stand for 2 or 3 minutes, then stir it to dissolve the yeast completely. Set the bowl in a warm, draft-free place, such as an unlighted oven, for 8 to 10 minutes, or until the yeast bubbles and doubles in bulk.

Place 4 cups of all-purpose flour (or 5¼ cups of granulated flour) in a large mixing bowl. Make a well in the center and add the yeast mixture, the cold milk, 1 tablespoon of butter, 2 eggs, salt, cardamom, vanilla and the remaining sugar. With your fingers, mix the ingredients together until a soft dough is formed, then shape into a ball and place it on a floured pastry cloth or board. To knead the dough pull it into an oblong shape, fold it end to end, then press it down and push it forward several times with the heels of the hands. Turn dough slightly toward you and repeat the process—pulling, folding, pushing and pressing. Continue kneading until the dough is smooth and elastic. This will take at least 10 minutes. Sprinkle the dough with flour, wrap in aluminum foil and refrigerate for 30 minutes.

Meanwhile, remove the butter from the refrigerator and let it soften to the point where it is neither too hard nor too soft; it should hold the impression of a finger. If the butter is in the shape of a brick, place it on a sheet of wax paper lightly dusted with flour, dust with more flour and cover with another sheet of wax paper. With a heavy rolling pin, roll the butter into an 8-by-12-inch rectangle, ¼ inch thick. Cut it in half, making 2 sheets, each a 6-by-8-inch rectangle. Wrap both halves in wax paper, and place in the refrigerator. If the butter has become very soft while rolling it, chill until it is again as firm as when you began rolling it, but it should not become hard. If the butter is in quarter-pound sticks, slice each quarter in half lengthwise. Place 4 of the pieces side by side on wax paper dusted with flour, dust with more flour and cover with another sheet of wax paper. With a heavy rolling pin, roll the butter into a rectangle 6 by 8 inches in size and ¼ inch thick. Repeat with the remaining butter.

Liberally sprinkle a pastry board or cloth (of canvas or heavy muslin) with flour. Roll the chilled dough out on the floured surface into a 9-by-18-

inch rectangle, 1/8 inch thick. Place 1 sheet of butter across the center of the dough and bring the end of the dough farther from you over the butter, sealing it along the sides with your fingers. Place the other sheet of butter on top and bring the other half of the dough over that, again sealing the butter in. Dust with flour, wrap in aluminum foil and chill 20 minutes.

Turn the dough around so that the narrow side faces you. Roll out the dough to an 8-by-18-inch strip. Fold both narrow ends in to meet at the center, then fold in half, making 4 layers. Wrap again in foil, chill another 20 minutes, and repeat the procedure—with the narrow side toward you, roll it out, fold it in 4 layers, then chill for 20 minutes. Remove from the refrigerator, roll into an 8-by-18-inch rectangle again, and finally fold it in half. Wrap in foil and chill 2 to 3 hours (or overnight) before using.

To make the butter cake *(page 76)*, use half the dough. To make the pastries *(page 73-75)*, use a quarter of the dough for each recipe. Even if you choose to use all the dough for only 1 type of pastry, cut it into quarters to facilitate handling.

Spandauer
ENVELOPES (DANISH)

To make 5 pastries

	2 tablespoons red currant jelly
1/4 Danish pastry dough *(page 72)*	1 tablespoon soft butter
1/3 cup pastry cream *(page 80)*	2 tablespoons flour

Preheat the oven to 400°. On a floured surface, roll the dough into a 4-by-20-inch rectangle. With a pastry wheel or small, sharp knife, trim the ragged edges of the dough and cut the rectangle into 5 parts, making 4-by-4-inch squares of dough. Fold in each corner to meet in the center, and press down the points to seal them. Place a heaping tablespoon of pastry cream in the center of each envelope and top with a teaspoon of red currant jelly. With a pastry brush or paper towel, grease a cookie sheet with 1 tablespoon of butter and sprinkle it with flour, tapping off any excess. Place the *spandauer* on the sheet and set in the middle of the oven for 10 minutes. Reduce the heat to 350° and bake 15 minutes, until the pastries are a light gold. With a wide spatula, transfer them to a wire cake rack to cool.

Snegle

SNAILS (DANISH)

To make 8 pastries

¼ Danish pastry dough *(page 72)*
1 egg white mixed with 1 teaspoon
   water
⅔ cup coarsely chopped walnuts

3 tablespoons sugar combined with
   1 tablespoon ground cinnamon
2 tablespoons dried black currants,
   soaked in 2 tablespoons Cognac
   or rum and drained
1 tablespoon soft butter
2 tablespoons flour

Preheat the oven to 400°. On a floured surface, roll the dough into a 9-by-16-inch rectangle. Brush lightly with the egg white and water mixture, then sprinkle with the chopped nuts, cinnamon-sugar mixture and currants. Place a sheet of wax paper on top and gently press the topping into the dough with a rolling pin. Peel off the wax paper and roll up the dough lengthwise, forming a 16-inch-long tight roll. Make 2 slits ½ inch apart, penetrating only ¾ of the way into the roll. Then cut all the way through the roll ½ inch past the partial cuts. (Each pastry will thus be 1½ inches long and have 2 slits in it.) Gently spread open each pastry until it resembles a fan. Grease a cookie sheet with 1 tablespoon of butter and sprinkle it with flour, tapping off any excess. Place the fans on the sheet and bake 10 minutes, then lower the heat to 350° and bake another 15 minutes. Remove from the oven and transfer the fans to a wire cake rack to cool.

Abrikossnitte

APRICOT SLIPS (DANISH)

To make 9 pastries

½ cup apricot preserve, rubbed
   through a sieve
¼ Danish pastry dough *(page 72)*

1 egg white combined with 1 teaspoon
   water
Coarse sugar
1 tablespoon soft butter
2 tablespoons flour

Preheat the oven to 400°. Cook the apricot preserve in a 1-quart enameled or stainless-steel saucepan over low heat, stirring almost constantly, until it has reduced to about 6 tablespoons. Set aside to cool.

On a floured surface, roll the dough into a 10-by-18-inch rectangle. With a pastry wheel or small, sharp knife, trim away its ragged edges. Using a spatula or the back of a spoon, spread half of the dough lengthwise with the apricot preserve. Carefully fold over the other half of the dough to form a long envelope. Dust the top with flour, place a sheet of wax paper on top, and, with a rolling pin, roll the dough gently to press in the filling. Peel off the wax paper and cut through the dough at 2-inch intervals, making 9 pastries 2 by 5 inches in size. With a small, sharp knife, make a 3-inch slit in the center of each pastry, leaving 1 inch unslit on either side. Bend one uncut end of the strip under the slit and, with your finger, push it up through the pastry to make a bow-tie-like shape. Lightly grease a cookie sheet with 1 tablespoon of butter and sprinkle it with flour, tapping off any excess flour. Set the pastries on the cookie sheet and brush them with the egg white and water. Sprinkle with sugar and bake 10 minutes. Reduce the heat to 350° and bake another 15 minutes. Remove from the oven and, with a wide spatula, transfer to a cake rack to cool.

Hanekam
COCKS' COMBS (DANISH)

To make 6 pastries

¼ Danish pastry dough *(page 72)*

FRANGIPANE FILLING
3 tablespoons unsalted butter
6 tablespoons almond paste
1 teaspoon flour
⅛ teaspoon grated lemon rind

1 egg white combined with 1 teaspoon
  water
Granulated sugar
1 tablespoon soft butter
2 tablespoons flour

To make the frangipane filling, cream the butter by using an electric mixer set at medium speed or by beating it against the side of a bowl with a wooden spoon. When light and fluffy, beat in the almond paste, a little at a time, and then the flour and grated lemon rind. Preheat the oven to 400°. On a floured surface, roll the dough into a 10-by-15-inch rectangle. With a pastry wheel or small, sharp knife, cut off its ragged edges. Spread a thin layer of the frangipane lengthwise over half of the dough. Fold the other side over, seal the edges with your fingers and cut into 2½-inch strips. Now cut 3 slits ¾ of the way into each strip, and bend the strips slightly so that they form a crescent. With a pastry brush or paper towel, grease a cookie sheet with 1 tablespoon of butter and sprinkle it with flour, tapping off any excess. Set the pastries on the sheet and brush each strip with the egg white and water mixture. Sprinkle with sugar and bake 10 minutes. Reduce the heat to 350° and bake another 10 minutes. Remove from the oven and, with a wide spatula, transfer the pastries to a wire cake rack to cool.

Smørkage
BUTTER CAKE (DANISH)

To make an 8- or 9-inch round cake

½ Danish pastry dough *(page 72)*	4 tablespoons unsalted butter
1 egg white combined with 1 teaspoon water	¼ cup sugar
	2 teaspoons almond extract

Cut off ⅓ of the dough and replace the other ⅔ in the refrigerator. On a floured pastry cloth or board, roll the small piece of dough into an 11- or 12-inch circle. Place the bottom of an 8- or 9-inch false-bottomed cake pan over the dough and with a sharp knife, cut the dough around the pan into a circle slightly larger than the pan (the dough tends to shrink when cut). Press the circle of dough into the bottom of the cake pan until it fits snugly, and brush with the egg white and water mixture.

Preheat the oven to 350°. Roll out the remaining ⅔ of the dough into a 14-by-14-inch square. Cream the 4 tablespoons of butter and the sugar by using an electric mixer set at medium speed or by beating them against the side of a bowl with a wooden spoon. Beat in the almond extract and spread this mixture over half of the dough. Fold over the other half so that the two ends meet. With a small, sharp knife, cut the dough at 2-inch intervals, making 7 strips each 2 by 7 inches in size. Roll up each strip lengthwise and tuck the flap under the roll. Stand up 6 of the rolls (tucked end under) around the border of the dough in the pan, and stand the last roll in the middle. Bake in the center of the oven for 45 minutes, or until the top is golden brown.

ICING

1 egg white	Pinch of salt
1½ cups sifted confectioners' sugar	1 teaspoon lemon juice

Meanwhile, make the icing. In a large mixing bowl, beat the egg white to a froth by hand or in an electric mixer, and then beat in the sugar, salt and lemon juice. Continue to beat until the mixture is light and fluffy and forms soft peaks when the beater is removed from the bowl. (If the icing in the bowl is covered with plastic wrap, it can be kept at room temperature for several days.) Remove the cake from the oven and while it is still warm, brush the entire surface with the icing.

Julekage

DANISH CHRISTMAS FRUIT LOAF

To make 1 large loaf

2 packages active dry yeast
¼ cup sugar
½ cup lukewarm milk (110° to 115°)
¼ teaspoon salt
½ teaspoon vanilla
½ teaspoon grated lemon rind
2 eggs, lightly beaten
½ teaspoon ground cardamom
3 to 4 cups all-purpose flour, sifted
1 cup mixed candied fruits (lemon, orange, cherry, pineapple)
1 tablespoon flour
8 tablespoons (1 quarter-pound stick) unsalted butter, softened

Sprinkle the yeast and 1 tablespoon of the sugar over the lukewarm milk. Let the mixture stand in the cup for 2 or 3 minutes, then stir gently to dissolve them. Set in a warm place, perhaps in an unlighted oven. When the yeast begins to bubble in about 8 to 10 minutes, stir it gently, and with a rubber spatula, transfer it to a large mixing bowl. Stir in the salt, vanilla, lemon rind, eggs, cardamom and the remaining sugar. Then add 3 cups of flour, a little at a time, stirring at first and then kneading with your hands until the dough becomes firm enough to be formed into a ball.

Shake the candied fruits in a small paper bag with 1 tablespoon of flour. (The flour will prevent the fruits from sticking together and enable them to disperse evenly throughout the dough.) Now add the fruits and the softened butter to the dough and knead for about 10 minutes, adding more flour, if necessary, to make the dough medium-soft. The finished dough should be shiny and elastic, and its surface blistered. Shape into a ball and place in a large buttered bowl. Dust the top lightly with flour, cover with a kitchen towel and set it in a warm, draft-free spot (again, an unlighted oven is ideal). In 45 minutes to 1 hour the dough should double in bulk and leave a deep depression when two fingers are pressed into the center.

After removing the dough, preheat the oven to 350°. Punch the dough down with your fists and knead again quickly. Shape it into a fat loaf and put it into a lightly buttered 1½-quart loaf pan. Cover again with the towel and let the dough rise in a warm spot for 15 to 20 minutes until it is almost double in bulk.

Bake the *julekage* in the center of the oven for 45 minutes. Remove the loaf from the pan and let it cool on a cake rack. It will keep well for 2 or 3 weeks if wrapped well in aluminum foil and refrigerated.

Mazarintårta

MAZARIN CAKE (SWEDISH)

To make one 8-inch round cake

PASTRY

1½ teaspoons sugar
¼ teaspoon salt
2 egg yolks
1⅓ cups all-purpose flour

8 tablespoons (1 quarter-pound
stick) unsalted butter, softened

TO MAKE THE PASTRY, cream the butter and sugar together by using an electric mixer set at medium speed or by beating them against the side of a bowl with a wooden spoon until light and fluffy. Beat in the salt and the egg yolks, 1 at a time. Now beat in the flour and mix well. Flour your hands lightly and shape the pastry into a ball. Wrap in wax paper and chill for at least 30 minutes.

FRANGIPANE FILLING

8 tablespoons (1 quarter-pound stick)
unsalted butter, softened
1 cup almond paste, at room
temperature
2 eggs, lightly beaten

1 teaspoon grated lemon rind
2 teaspoons flour

1 tablespoon butter, softened
Confectioners' sugar

TO MAKE THE FRANGIPANE, cream the butter by using an electric mixer set at medium speed or by beating it against the side of a bowl with a wooden spoon until it is light and fluffy. Beat in the almond paste, 2 tablespoons at a time, and then beat in the lightly beaten eggs. Continue to beat until the mixture is very smooth, then stir in the grated lemon rind and flour. Set aside.

Preheat the oven to 325°. Place the chilled dough on a floured board or pastry cloth. Dust a little flour over it and roll it out—from the center to within an inch of the far edge. Lift the dough and turn it clockwise, about the space of 2 hours on the clock; roll again from the center to the far edge. Repeat—lifting, turning, rolling—until you make a circle 11 or 12 inches in diameter and about ⅛ inch thick. Butter the bottom and sides of an 8-inch false-bottomed cake pan with the tablespoon of softened butter.

Roll the pastry over the pin and unroll it over the pan, or drape the pastry over the rolling pin, lift it up and unfold it over the pan. Gently press the pastry into the bottom and around the sides of the pan, being careful not to stretch it. Roll the pin over the rim of the pan, pressing down hard to trim off the excess pastry. With a rubber spatula, spread the filling on top of the pastry.

Place the cake pan in the center of the oven for 45 to 50 minutes, or until the pastry is golden brown and the filling is set. Let the cake cool a little in the pan, then set the pan on a large jar or coffee can and slip down the outside rim. Slide the cake onto a platter, sprinkle with confectioners' sugar, and serve at room temperature.

Kermakakku
SOUR-CREAM POUNDCAKE (FINNISH)

To make 1 loaf

2 teaspoons unsalted butter, softened
1 tablespoon dry bread crumbs
8 tablespoons (1 quarter-pound stick) unsalted butter, softened
1 cup sugar
3 eggs

1¾ cups all-purpose flour
1 teaspoon baking soda
½ teaspoon cinnamon
1 teaspoon ground cardamom or substitute ground ginger
1 cup sour cream
1 teaspoon vanilla

With a pastry brush or paper towels, grease a 9-by-5-by-3 loaf pan with 2 teaspoons of soft butter, and sprinkle the bottom and sides of the pan with bread crumbs; tap out any excess crumbs. Preheat the oven to 350°.

Cream the ¼ pound of butter and sugar together by using an electric mixer set at medium speed or by beating them vigorously against the sides of the bowl with a wooden spoon until the mixture is light and fluffy. Beat in the eggs, one at a time, making sure each is thoroughly mixed in before adding another. Sift together the flour, baking soda, cinnamon and cardamom (or ginger) and stir half of it into the batter. Beat in the sour cream and vanilla, and when all these ingredients are well combined, beat in the rest of the flour.

With the aid of a rubber spatula, pour the contents of the bowl into the prepared loaf pan and rap the pan sharply on the table once to remove any air pockets. Bake in the center of the oven for 50 to 60 minutes, or until the top of the cake is golden brown and is lightly springy to the touch. Test further by inserting a toothpick in the center of the cake; it should come out dry and clean. Remove from the oven and run a knife around the cake to loosen it from the pan. Place a wire cake rack on top of the pan and invert the two; then place a second cake rack on top of the cake and again invert, so that the cake is now right side up. Cool the cake on the rack and serve at room temperature.

Operatårta

CREAMY LAYER CAKE (SWEDISH)

To make 1 cake

SPONGECAKE
2 tablespoons soft butter
2 tablespoons flour
4 egg whites

¼ cup sugar
4 egg yolks
½ teaspoon vanilla
¼ cup sifted cornstarch
¼ cup sifted flour

Preheat the oven to 400°. Spread an 11-by-16-inch jelly-roll pan with 1 tablespoon of the soft butter and line the pan with a 22-inch strip of wax paper, letting the wax paper extend over the narrower ends of the pan. Similarly spread the wax paper with the remaining soft butter, then sprinkle it with the 2 tablespoons of flour and tip it from side to side to be sure the surface is evenly covered. Knock out any excess flour.

In a large mixing bowl (preferably of unlined copper), beat the egg whites with a large balloon whisk, rotary or electric beater until they form soft peaks. Gradually beat in the sugar, 1 tablespoon at a time, and continue to beat vigorously until the egg whites form stiff, unwavering peaks. Place the egg yolks in another large mixing bowl and stir them gently for a minute or so; then stir in the vanilla. With a rubber spatula, mix a heaping tablespoon of the beaten egg whites into the yolks, then pour the mixture over the remaining egg whites in the bowl and sprinkle with the cornstarch and flour. Fold all of the ingredients together gently, using an under-over motion rather than a rotary motion. When the egg whites are no longer visible, pour the mixture into the already prepared jelly-roll pan and spread it out evenly and gently with a rubber spatula. Bake for 10 to 12 minutes, or until the cake is a light golden brown. Remove the pan from the oven, loosen the sides of the cake with a metal spatula or knife and, using the ends of the wax paper as handles, lift it out of the pan. Turn it over onto wax paper to cool and carefully peel off the original wax paper.

PASTRY CREAM
¼ cup flour
2 cups light cream
¼ teaspoon salt
¾ cup sugar
8 egg yolks

2 teaspoons vanilla
1 package powdered unflavored gelatin, softened for 3 minutes in ¼ cup cold water

¾ cup sliced blanched almonds

While the cake is cooling, prepare the pastry cream. In a 1½- to 2-quart enameled or stainless-steel saucepan, vigorously beat the ¼ cup flour and ½ cup of the light cream into a smooth paste with a wire whisk. Then gradually beat in the rest of the cream, salt and sugar. Cook over moderate heat, still beating vigorously, for 1 or 2 minutes, or until the mixture is thick and smooth. Remove from the heat.

In a small bowl combine ¼ cup of the hot sauce with the egg yolks. Then slowly pour this mixture in a thin stream into the pan, whisking constantly. Cook over low heat for 1 or 2 minutes, stirring all the time, but do not let it boil. Remove from the heat and stir in the vanilla, and then the softened gelatin. Set the pastry cream aside to cool.

When the spongecake has cooled to room temperature, slice it crosswise into 3 equal parts (each measuring 11 by 5 inches). Place 1 layer on a flat serving platter and spread ¼ of the cooled pastry cream over it with a spatula or spoon. Place the second layer of cake on top and spread with another ¼ of the pastry cream. Top with the remaining cake and spread the top and sides with the remaining pastry cream. With your fingertips or a piece of wax paper, gently press the sliced almonds into the pastry cream all around and on top of the cake. Chill for at least 2 hours before serving.

Toscatårta

ALMOND-TOPPED CAKE (SWEDISH)

To make one 8-inch round cake

CAKE

2 teaspoons unsalted butter, softened
1 tablespoon dry bread crumbs

1 cup all-purpose flour
1 teaspoon double-acting baking
   powder

¼ teaspoon salt
2 eggs
⅔ cup sugar
½ teaspoon vanilla
¼ cup milk
4 tablespoons unsalted butter, melted

Preheat the oven to 350°. With a pastry brush or a paper towel, spread the bottom and sides of an 8-inch round pan with 2 teaspoons of soft butter, then sprinkle with bread crumbs. Turn the pan over and tap out any excess crumbs.

Sift the flour, baking powder and salt together in a mixing bowl. In another large bowl, beat the eggs with a wire whisk, rotary or electric beater until they are well blended. Slowly beat in the sugar and vanilla and continue to beat until the mixture falls back into the bowl in a lazy ribbon when the whisk or beater is lifted out.

With a rubber spatula, fold the flour mixture and milk alternately into the eggs and sugar by first adding about ⅓ of the flour, then a little milk, then another ⅓ of flour, the remaining milk, and last, the remaining flour. (Fold by using a slow under-over motion rather than a rotary motion.) Before the last of the flour has been folded into the batter, add the melted butter. As soon as there is no further trace of either flour or butter, pour the batter into the prepared pan. Be careful not to overfold. Rap the pan sharply on the table once to remove any air pockets.

Bake the cake in the center of the oven for 30 to 40 minutes, or until the cake is golden brown and is springy when touched lightly. Test further by inserting a toothpick into the center of the cake; it should come out dry and clean.

ALMOND TOPPING

2 tablespoons unsalted butter, softened
¼ cup sugar
1 tablespoon flour

2 tablespoons milk
⅓ cup sliced blanched almonds
½ teaspoon vanilla

Meanwhile, prepare the almond topping. Combine the butter, sugar and flour in a small pan and stir together briefly with a wooden spoon. Add the milk and cook over low heat, stirring constantly, for 2 or 3 minutes, until the mixture is smooth and thick. Remove from the heat and stir in the almonds and vanilla. Set aside.

Preheat the broiler to its lowest level. When the cake is done, carefully run a knife around the edge to loosen it from the pan; then place a wire cake rack on top and invert the two. Set another rack on top of the cake and again invert; the top of the cake is now facing up. With an icing spatula or spoon, spread the topping lightly and evenly over the hot cake. Place the cake, still on its rack, under the broiler, about 3 inches from the heat. Broil 3 to 5 minutes, until the top is golden brown and bubbling. Check constantly to be sure that the topping does not burn. Serve while still warm.

Sandkage

SAND CAKE (DANISH)

To make one 8-inch round cake

2 teaspoons unsalted butter, softened
1 tablespoon dry bread crumbs
16 tablespoons (2 quarter-pound sticks) unsalted butter
1 cup sugar
4 eggs, at room temperature

1 tablespoon brandy
1 teaspoon vanilla
1 teaspoon grated lemon rind
2 cups all-purpose flour
1 tablespoon cornstarch
¼ teaspoon salt
2¼ teaspoons double-acting baking powder

Preheat the oven to 350°. With a pastry brush or a paper towel, lightly spread the bottom and sides of an 8-inch tube pan (including the inner cone of the pan) with the 2 teaspoons of soft butter. Sprinkle the bottom and sides of the pan evenly with bread crumbs, turn the pan over and tap out any excess crumbs.

Cream the ½ pound of butter and sugar together with an electric mixer set at medium speed or by beating them against the sides of a bowl with a wooden spoon until very light and fluffy. Now beat in the 4 eggs, 1 at a time, making sure that each one is thoroughly incorporated before adding another. Then beat in the tablespoon of brandy, teaspoon of vanilla and teaspoon of grated lemon rind. Should the mixture appear to be curdling, beat it very hard until it becomes smooth again. Sift the flour, cornstarch, salt and baking powder together into a mixing bowl and add them to the butter-egg mixture all at once. Beat vigorously until the ingredients are all absorbed, but no longer.

Pour the batter into the prepared tube pan. Rap the pan once sharply on the table to eliminate any air pockets, and bake in the center of the oven for 50 to 60 minutes, or until the top is golden brown and springy when lightly touched. Run a knife around the edge of the cake to loosen it from the pan; then place a wire cake rack on top of the cake and invert the two. Set another rack on top of the cake and again invert, so that the top of the cake is now facing up. Serve at room temperature.

Suomalaisleipä

FINNISH BREAD

To make 1 loaf

4 packages active dry yeast	1½ teaspoons salt
3 teaspoons dark brown sugar	2 cups all-purpose flour
1¼ cups lukewarm water	1½ cups rye flour
1 tablespoon melted butter	1 tablespoon soft butter

Sprinkle the yeast and 1 teaspoon of the brown sugar over ½ cup of the luke-warm water. Be absolutely sure that the water is lukewarm—neither too hot nor too cool to the touch. Let the mixture stand for 2 or 3 minutes, then stir it to dissolve the yeast completely. Set the cup aside in a warm, draft-free spot (such as an unlighted oven) for 5 to 7 minutes, or until the mixture has begun to bubble and has almost doubled in volume.

Pour the yeast mixture into a large mixing bowl, add the remaining ¾ cup of lukewarm water, and, with a wooden spoon, mix in the remaining 2 teaspoons of brown sugar, the melted butter, salt, white flour and 1 cup of the rye flour. When the mixture forms a smooth dough, gather it into a ball, cover the bowl loosely with a kitchen towel and let it rest at room temper-ature for about 10 minutes.

Transfer the dough to a floured pastry cloth or board and knead it by pulling the dough into an oblong shape, folding it end to end, then press-ing it down and pushing it forward several times with the heels of your hands. Turn the dough slightly toward you and repeat the process—pulling, folding, pushing and pressing. Continue to knead, using the extra ½ cup of rye flour to sprinkle over the dough and pastry board or cloth if either becomes sticky.

When the dough is elastic and smooth, gather it into a rough ball and place it in a large, lightly buttered bowl. Dust the top of the dough lightly with flour, cover it again with the kitchen towel and let it rest in the warm, draft-free spot (the oven, again) for about 45 minutes, until it has doubled in bulk and no longer springs back when it is poked with a finger.

Preheat the oven to 375°. With a pastry brush or paper towel, lightly spread a cookie sheet with the tablespoon of soft butter and sprinkle it with flour, tipping the sheet to coat it evenly. Turn it over and tap it on a hard surface to knock off any excess flour. Punch the dough down with your fist, and knead it again briefly on the pastry board. Shape it into a round, flat loaf about 9 or 10 inches in diameter, and set on the cookie sheet. Bake 1 hour, or until the bread has a dark-brown crust and a toothpick or skewer inserted in its center comes out dry and clean. Remove to a cake rack to cool, and serve, if possible, while still warm.

Beverages

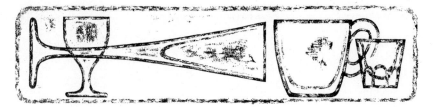

Professorns Glögg
THE PROFESSOR'S GLÖGG (SWEDISH)

To serve 20 to 25

2 quarts dry red wine
2 quarts muscatel
1 pint sweet vermouth
2 tablespoons Angostura bitters
2 cups raisins
Peelings of 1 orange
12 whole cardamoms, bruised in a
   mortar with a pestle or by covering
with a towel and crushing with a
   rolling pin
10 whole cloves
1 piece (about 2 inches) fresh ginger
1 stick cinnamon
1½ cups (12 ounces) aquavit
1½ cups sugar
2 cups whole almonds, blanched and
   peeled

In a 6- to 8-quart enameled or stainless-steel pot, mix together the dry red wine, muscatel, sweet vermouth, bitters, raisins, orange peel and the slightly crushed cardamoms, whole cloves, ginger and cinnamon. Cover and let the mixture stand at least 12 hours so that the flavors will develop and mingle. Shortly before serving, add the aquavit and the sugar. Stir well and bring it to a full boil over high heat. Remove at once from the heat, stir in the almonds and serve the hot *glögg* in mugs. In Sweden, a small spoon is placed in each mug to scoop up the almonds and raisins.

ALTERNATE: To make a simpler *glögg*, divide the quantities of spices in half and mix them with 2 bottles of dry red wine. Leave it overnight, then stir in ¾ cup of sugar and bring almost to a boil. Remove from the heat, stir in 1 cup of whole, blanched and peeled almonds, and serve hot.

Sima

LEMON-FLAVORED MEAD (FINNISH)

To make 5 quarts

2 large lemons
½ cup plus 5 teaspoons granulated
    sugar

½ cup brown sugar
5 quarts boiling water
⅛ teaspoon active dry yeast
15 raisins

With a small, sharp knife or rotary peeler, carefully peel off the yellow skins of the lemons and set them aside. Then cut away the white membranes of the lemons and discard them. Slice the lemons very thinly. In a 6- to 8-quart enameled or stainless-steel bowl, combine the lemon slices, lemon skins, the ½ cup granulated sugar and the brown sugar. Pour the boiling water over the fruit and sugar, stir, and let the mixture cool to tepid. Then stir in the yeast. Allow the *sima* to ferment, uncovered, at room temperature for about 12 hours. To bottle, use 5 one-quart bottles with very tight covers or corks. Place 1 teaspoon of sugar and 3 raisins in the bottom of each bottle. Strain the *sima* through a sieve and, using a funnel, pour the liquid into the bottles. Close the bottles tightly and let them stand at room temperature for 1 or 2 days until the raisins have risen to the surface. Chill the sealed bottles until ready to serve.

Recipe Index: English

Recipe Index: Scandinavian

Notes

Illustrations by Matt Greene